THE CONTEXT OF MILITARY ENVIRONMENTS

An Agenda for Basic Research on Social and Organizational Factors Relevant to Small Units

Committee on the Context of Military Environments:
Social and Organizational Factors

Board on Behavioral, Cognitive, and Sensory Sciences

Division of Behavioral and Social Sciences and Education

NATIONAL RESEARCH COUNCIL
OF THE NATIONAL ACADEMIES

THE NATIONAL ACADEMIES PRESS
Washington, D.C.
www.nap.edu

THE NATIONAL ACADEMIES PRESS 500 Fifth Street, NW Washington, DC 20001

NOTICE: The project that is the subject of this report was approved by the Governing Board of the National Research Council, whose members are drawn from the councils of the National Academy of Sciences, the National Academy of Engineering, and the Institute of Medicine. The members of the committee responsible for the report were chosen for their special competences and with regard for appropriate balance.

This study was supported by Contract/Grant No. W911NF-12-1-0514 between the National Academy of Sciences and the Department of the Army. Any opinions, findings, conclusions, or recommendations expressed in this publication are those of the author(s) and do not necessarily reflect the views of the organizations or agencies that provided support for the project.

International Standard Book Number-13: 978-0-309-30684-3
International Standard Book Number-10: 0-309-30684-1

Additional copies of this report are available from the National Academies Press, 500 Fifth Street, NW, Keck 360, Washington, DC 20001; (800) 624-6242 or (202) 334-3313; http://www.nap.edu.

Printed in the United States of America

Cover credits: Top: U.S. Army Pfc. Amy Alexanders dresses in her Marne Standard battle gear before taking part in a physical demands study, February 2014, photo by the Associated Press. Bottom: Army graphic from the Army Doctrine Reference Policy–P. 1-10, ADRP 3-0.

Suggested citation: National Research Council. (2014). *The Context of Military Environments: An Agenda for Basic Research on Social and Organizational Factors Relevant to Small Units.* Committee on the Context of Military Environments: Social and Organizational Factors, Board on Behavioral, Cognitive, and Sensory Sciences, Division of Behavioral and Social Sciences and Education. Washington, DC: The National Academies Press.

COMMITTEE ON THE CONTEXT OF MILITARY ENVIRONMENTS: SOCIAL AND ORGANIZATIONAL FACTORS

REID HASTIE (*Chair*), Chicago Booth Business School, University of Chicago
CATHERINE H. TINSLEY (*Vice Chair*), McDonough School of Business, Georgetown University
BURT S. BARNOW, Trachtenberg School of Public Policy and Public Administration, The George Washington University
CORINNE BENDERSKY, Anderson School of Management, University of California, Los Angeles
EDWARD J. COSS, U.S. Army Command and General Staff College
LESLIE A. DECHURCH, School of Psychology, Georgia Institute of Technology
JONATHAN GRATCH, Department of Computer Science, Psychology, and Institute for Creative Technologies, University of Southern California
DOUGLAS H. HARRIS, Anacapa Sciences, Inc., Santa Barbara, CA
LEE D. HOFFER, Department of Anthropology, Case Western Reserve University
ALAIR MACLEAN, Department of Sociology, Washington State University, Vancouver
CHARLES F. MANSKI, Department of Economics and Institute for Policy Research, Northwestern University
ROBERT S. RUSH,[1] Office of the Surgeon General of the Army
JEFFREY SANCHEZ-BURKS,[2] Ross School of Business, University of Michigan
WILLIAM SCHULZE, Charles H. Dyson School of Applied Economics and Management, Cornell University

CHERIE CHAUVIN, *Study Director*
TINA M. WINTERS, *Associate Program Officer*
RENÉE L. WILSON GAINES, *Senior Program Assistant*

[1]Resigned April 2014
[2]Resigned April 2013

Preface

Near the end of 2011, the U.S. Army Research Institute for the Behavioral and Social Sciences (ARI) approached the National Research Council (NRC) to establish a committee to synthesize and assess basic research opportunities in the behavioral and social sciences related to social and organizational factors that comprise the context of individual and small unit behavior in military environments.

In response to the request from ARI, the NRC established the Committee on the Context of Military Environments: Social and Organizational Factors, under the oversight of the Board on Behavioral, Cognitive, and Sensory Sciences. This report is the work of that committee. To some extent, this report is a follow-up to the 2008 NRC report, *Human Behavior in Military Contexts,* which also was requested by ARI. Whereas the 2008 report focused on individual attributes that affect human behavior, the current study and its report focus on contextual forces, specifically social and organizational factors, that influence individual and small unit behavior.

Members of the committee were volunteers, carefully selected by the NRC to cover a spectrum of relevant academic specialties and to bring expertise in both basic research and practical applications in diverse settings, including private organizations, government, and the military. Several committee members have had significant experience with military environments, including overseas deployments and longer-term assignments.

The study extended over a 24-month period, during which the committee met a total of four times. In its data-gathering sessions, the committee received briefings from current and former military service members (representing a wide range of ranks, occupational specialties, and experiences), as well as from researchers with military expertise and expertise in parallel areas of research with potential relevance to the committee's charge. These briefings provided the committee with critical context to assess a potential research agenda to address military needs, given the unique missions, challenges, and environments of military units.

Throughout its deliberations, the committee considered multiple military environments within which service members are regularly required to operate—and within which they are likely to continue to operate, well into the future. The recommendations developed in Chapters 1 through 7 and compiled in Chapter 8 of this report propose a research agenda that is both important and feasible, given the future environments the military is likely to face.

Reid Hastie, *Chair*
Catherine H. Tinsley, *Vice Chair*
Cherie Chauvin, *Study Director*
Committee on the Context of Military Environments:
Social and Organizational Factors

Acknowledgments

This study was sponsored by the U.S. Army Research Institute for the Behavioral and Social Sciences (ARI). The committee is grateful to the many ARI staff members who made valuable contributions during committee meetings and provided informative materials to assist the committee's data-gathering process. Special thanks are due to Gerald (Jay) Goodwin, chief, Foundational Science Research Unit, ARI, for his vision, passion, and assistance in making this study a reality. Also special thanks go to Paul Gade of George Washington University, and formerly at ARI, for his expertise and guidance throughout the development and course of this study.

The committee benefited tremendously from expert presentations during its first two committee meetings by the following invited guests: Noshir Contractor, Northwestern University; Jessica Gallus, ARI; LTG Hank Hatch, U.S. Army, retired; Arwen Hunter, ARI; Robert Love, National Research Council; Betty Maxfield, Office of Army Demographics; David Segal, University of Maryland; MAJ John Spencer, U.S. Army G1; and LTC Eric J. Weis, U.S. Military Academy at West Point. The committee also had the unique opportunity to engage in roundtable and small group discussions with active and recently separated military service members. Their practical expertise living and working in various U.S. Army military environments provided crucial perspective to the committee's work. We thank the following individuals for their time, insight, and candor: from the U.S. Army, MAJ Brian Gellman; CWO4 Dwayn Hanford (retired); 1SG Donald Ingels (retired); CPT Patrick Jones; CPT Kelley Keating; CPT Kristin Marin; CPT Barron Moffitt; CPT Everage B. Robinson; MAJ John Spencer; SFC Paul Stier (retired); CPT Gerald Wynn; and LTC William Zana; as well as

CSM Alan Ferris of the U.S. Army National Guard and SMS Rob Hicks of the U.S. Air Force. We also thank CPT Andrew Miller, former U.S. Army, and MAJ Benjamin Tupper, U.S. Army National Guard, for their written contributions to assist the committee in understanding the operations of military teams across different environments. The committee also benefited from the expertise of Andrea B. Hollingshead and Peter J. Carnevale, University of Southern California, who authored a paper on emerging technical advances for application in behavioral studies of teams. And finally, we thank Susan T. Fiske, Princeton University, appointed as an external consultant to the committee, for her contribution to the committee deliberations and for review of early drafts of the report.

Among the National Research Council (NRC) staff, special thanks are due to Barbara A. Wanchisen, director, Board on Behavioral, Cognitive, and Sensory Sciences, who provided oversight and support of the study from its initial development through to the release of this final report. Tina Winters, associate program officer, also provided critical support to the committee's data gathering, deliberations, and development of the final report. Additionally, Renée L. Wilson Gaines, senior program assistant, provided administrative and logistic support over the course of the study to ensure the needs of the committee and its guests were fulfilled without exception. And Jatryce Jackson, program associate, provided valuable assistance through the final stages of report preparation. Ellen Kimmel and Rebecca Morgan, of the NRC Research Center, contributed extensive research support throughout the entire study process. And finally we thank the executive office reports staff of the Division of Behavioral and Social Sciences and Education, especially Kirsten Sampson Snyder, who managed the report review process; Robert Katt (consultant), who performed preliminary and final editing of the report; and Yvonne Wise, who provided valuable help with production of the report.

This report has been reviewed in draft form by individuals chosen for their diverse perspectives and technical expertise, in accordance with procedures approved by the NRC's Report Review Committee. The purpose of this independent review is to provide candid and critical comments that will assist the institution in making its published report as sound as possible and to ensure that the report meets institutional standards for objectivity, evidence, and responsiveness to the study charge. The review comments and draft manuscript remain confidential to protect the integrity of the deliberative process. We wish to thank the following individuals for their review of this report: CPT Roxanne E. Bras, Defense Entrepreneurs Forum, U.S. Army; Michael Drillings, MANPRINT, U.S. Army; Alice H. Eagly, Institute for Policy Research, Department of Psychology, Northwestern University; LTC(MP) Eugenia K. Guilmartin, Office of the Provost Marshall General, Policy and Plans, U.S. Army; CSM Michael Hall, retired,

U.S. Army, McChrystal Group; Christine Horne, Department of Sociology, Washington State University; Shelly M. MacDermid Wadsworth, Military Family Research Institute, Purdue University; Douglas S. Massey, Woodrow Wilson School of Public and International Affairs, Princeton University; John Mathieu, School of Business, University of Connecticut; Robert A. Rubinstein, Maxwell School, Syracuse University; Stephen Stark, Department of Psychology, University of South Florida; LTC Eric Weis, Simon Center for the Professional Military Ethic, U.S. Military Academy West Point; and Kelly A. Wolgast, Healthcare Leadership Program, Vanderbilt University School of Nursing.

Although the reviewers listed above provided many constructive comments and suggestions, they were not asked to endorse the content of the report nor did they see the final draft of the report before its release. The review of this report was overseen by Arthur Lupia, Institute for Social Research, University of Michigan, and Stephen M. Robinson, Department of Industrial and Systems Engineering, University of Wisconsin–Madison (*Emeritus*). Appointed by the National Research Council, they were responsible for making certain that an independent examination of this report was carried out in accordance with institutional procedures and that all review comments were carefully considered. Responsibility for the final content of this report rests entirely with the authoring committee and the institution. And for their work, we thank the committee members, all of whom took active roles in the study—in drafting chapters and leading discussions, and, most of all, in contributing their knowledge to this challenging task.

Reid Hastie, *Chair*
Catherine H. Tinsley, *Vice Chair*
Cherie Chauvin, *Study Director*
Committee on the Context of Military Environments:
Social and Organizational Factors

Contents

Summary

The U.S. Army faces a variety of challenges to maintain a ready and capable force into the future. Its missions are diverse, following a continuum from peace to war that includes combat and counterinsurgency operations as well as negotiation, reconstruction, and stability operations that require a variety of personnel and skill sets to execute. Missions often demand rapid decision making and coordination with others in novel ways, so that personnel are not simply following a specific set of tactical orders but, rather, carrying out mission command through an understanding of broader strategic goals in order to develop and choose among courses of action. Like any workforce, the Army is diverse in terms of demographic characteristics, such as gender and race, with a commitment of its leadership to ensure equal opportunities across all demographic parties. With these challenges comes the urgent need to better understand how contextual factors influence soldier and small unit behavior and mission performance.

Soldiers are embedded in several different contexts, each of which includes social and organizational factors. First is the context of their small unit: the team, squad, and platoon to which they are assigned. Second is the context of the larger Army organization, such as their battalion. Third is the context of their physical location and environment. They can be stationed with family (either in the United States or outside). They can be stationed on or off a military facility. They can be stationed in combat or noncombat environments. All these contexts can influence on how a soldier and his or her small unit operate.

Questions related to contextual factors have great bearing on issues of enduring concern to the military. For example, how do soldiers respond to

Army policy that seeks to change norms? How do organizational factors impact service members' resilience and operational effectiveness in the face of environmental transitions? How can leaders influence the social interactions within their units to foster environments of productive behavior?

Hence, the U.S. Army Research Institute for the Behavioral and Social Sciences (ARI) asked the National Research Council to convene an interdisciplinary group of experts "to synthesize and assess basic research opportunities in the behavioral and social sciences related to social and organizational factors that comprise the context of individual and small unit behavior in military environments." The study was to consider "tactical operations of small units and their leaders, to include the full spectrum of unique military environments."

Based on a careful review and collation of data from a diverse array of sources, the committee arrived at three key points.

First, ARI should play a more active role in making data on actual Army units available, and it should provide access for behavioral and social science researchers who want to study basic scientific questions in actual Army contexts and with actual soldiers and their data. Like most definitions of "basic research," ARI's definition is predicated on the idea of developing fundamental knowledge of phenomena without specific application in process or products. Yet, this definition does not preclude research on active duty soldiers in real military contexts. Since basic research aimed at understanding the impact of social and organizational context necessitates studies situated in the relevant context, it is the committee's opinion that allowing behavioral researchers access to active duty soldiers in military contexts is crucial. Furthermore, ARI should also facilitate access in order for researchers to integrate or synthesize data that have already been collected.

Recommendation 1
The committee strongly recommends that the Department of the Army support an appropriate mix of intramural and extramural basic scientific research on relevant Army personnel in military environments. The U.S. Army Research Institute for the Behavioral and Social Sciences (ARI) should be responsible for making appropriate data on Army units available and for promoting access for both internal and external behavioral researchers to study basic scientific questions in military contexts. ARI should increase its role as a facilitator or gateway for basic behavioral research in military contexts.

Second, a concerted research effort should be directed at developing unit-level measurements (in contrast to measures that aggregate individual-level assessments) of social and organizational factors. For example, methods should be developed to assign meaningful scores to a platoon to summarize the effectiveness of troops' understanding of leaders' intent (lieutenant, sergeant), and leaders' understanding of their troops' readiness and motivation. Through the course of this study, several critical areas emerged as particularly relevant for understanding social and organizational factors in the current and future Army missions. To develop fundamental knowledge in these critical research areas, the committee's recommendations call for ARI and other relevant U.S. military funding agencies to fund basic research that addresses questions related to norms, environmental transitions, contextual leadership, power and status hierarchies, and multiteam systems. Each area is presented in a separate chapter in this report as follows:

- How to understand the content, emergence, influence, and malleability of social norms (Chapter 2);
- How continual and repeated environmental transitions (e.g., deployments or reassignments) impact institutional routines and individual habits, with consequences for soldier resilience (Chapter 3);
- Contextual leadership, whereby leaders play a critical role in influencing the social context and thereby shape positive individual behavior and effective unit performance (Chapter 4);
- Status (e.g., informal processes of negotiating or obtaining respect and admiration from peers and subordinates) as an important source of influence in military units in addition to formal power, with substantial small unit performance implications (Chapter 5); and
- Multiteam systems, whereby personnel in military environments often work within teams of teams; including consideration of the potential benefits of developing unit-level measurements (in contrast to purely individual-level assessments) of the social variables critical to understanding the team-level and system-level domains (Chapter 6).

Third, the committee advocates the creation of a longitudinal database (Chapter 7) to include data collected from a probability sample of all recruits (with data providing a record of career paths and achievements for recruits from all backgrounds). The committee's recommendation focuses on the demographic and administrative requirements for a probability sample appropriate for this longitudinal cohort study and also calls for the U.S. military to expand the demographic and socioeconomic information collected from potential recruits during the application process. The committee also calls for active efforts to promote research using data from the Millennium Cohort Study, Global Assessment Tool (through the Army's

Comprehensive Soldier and Family Fitness Program), and other administrative records collected by the Department of Defense. The combined sets of data could provide a record of career paths and achievements for recruits from all backgrounds.

In addition, a new longitudinal survey, also described in Chapter 7, eliciting individual responses should be conducted periodically over the course of each soldier's career (including time both in and out of the armed forces) to obtain more detailed information about beliefs, attitudes, and experiences. The specific questions to be surveyed would be determined by a working group of ARI staff and other relevant experts in survey research and empirical social science. The committee stresses the unique opportunity the Army has to answer some basic behavioral and social science research questions on who advances and why—given the special characteristics of Army careers, such as promotion from within the ranks and large numbers of well-defined, comparable personnel positions. Therefore, the committee's final recommendation is a strong endorsement for creating and maintaining such a survey.

Recommendation 7.3
The U.S. Army Research Institute for the Behavioral and Social Sciences should establish a working group of experts in survey research, empirical social science, and military subject matter charged with development of a new longitudinal survey strategy to track both individuals and small units over time.

The committee was also asked to comment on the level of funding necessary to implement the recommended research agenda. In lieu of providing a specific funding level, the committee offers guidance to the Assistant Secretary of the Army for Acquisition, Logistics, and Technology (see Chapter 1) when considering appropriate funding levels for ARI basic research over the next 10 or more years. If limitations on funding necessitate ARI having to choose between breadth and depth (i.e., small allocations of funding across all of the initiatives featured in the recommended research agenda versus larger funding allocations within a portion of the recommended initiatives), the committee believes that opting for depth over breadth would yield more valuable knowledge gains. This is based on the members' collective research experience across several domains.

Rigorous research on the social and organizational factors that influence the behavior of soldiers and small units will contribute to the fundamental knowledge base needed to ensure that the U.S. Army can successfully address current and future challenges.

1

Introduction and Framework for Research Agenda

INTRODUCTION

The full spectrum of military environments experienced by today's soldiers includes many significant contextual forces that influence perceptions and behavior—both positively and negatively. It is well known that soldiers, as individuals and members of small units, possess attributes (e.g., mental health, intelligence, knowledge, and skills) that influence their behaviors. But it is less understood how social and organizational factors in the military context also influence those behaviors. To maximize the effectiveness of U.S. Army personnel policies and practices, the Army should seek to understand better how various social and organizational factors affect soldiers. This report describes innovative research programs that can be implemented to increase fundamental scientific and practical knowledge of Army soldiers and small units—and of the social and organizational factors in environments in which the Army operates—to enhance soldier and unit performance and capacities.

Study Overview

Recognizing the need to develop a portfolio of research to better understand the influence of social and organizational factors on the behavior of individuals and small units, the U.S. Army Research Institute for the Behavioral and Social Sciences (ARI) requested that the National Research Council's (NRC) Board on Behavioral, Cognitive, and Sensory Sciences establish an ad hoc committee to outline a productive and innovative collection of future basic science research projects to improve Army mission performance (see Statement of Task in Box 1-1). ARI's request sought a research agenda designed for immediate implementation and lasting over the next 10-20 years. In many ways this study was designed to build upon the foundation of the 2008 NRC report, *Human Behavior in Military Contexts* (National Research Council, 2008). However, the current study's emphasis shifts from that of individual soldier attributes—for example, intercultural competence, nonverbal behavior, emotion, and neurophysiology—to a more contextual approach to understand the influence of social and organizational factors on individual and small unit behavior. This report presents

Box 1-1
Statement of Task for the National Research Council Study

An ad-hoc committee of inter-disciplinary experts will synthesize and assess basic research opportunities in the behavioral and social sciences related to social and organizational factors that comprise the context of individual and small unit behavior in military environments. The committee will focus on tactical operations of small units and their leaders, to include the full spectrum of unique military environments including, for example, major combat operations, stability/support operations, peacekeeping, and military observer missions, as well as headquarters support units. Based on a careful review and collation of a variety of data, the committee will:

1. Identify key contextual factors that shape individual and small unit behavior. Assess the state of the science regarding these factors. Specifically, the committee will assess whether there are recent or emerging theoretical, technological, and/or statistical advances that have enabled or may enable new approaches and/or measurement capabilities to better understand social and organizational factors.

2. Recommend an agenda for U.S. Army Research Institute's (ARI) future research in order to maximize the effectiveness of U.S. Army personnel policies and practices (e.g., initial processes of selection, recruitment, and assignment as well as career development practices in training and leadership development). This is related to contextual factors that influence individual and small unit behavior (including, but not limited, to task/situation, team, organizational, cultural, societal, and life cohort factors). In developing this research agenda, the committee will identify immediate research opportunities in the most promising topics; that is, those which are likely to have the highest near-term payoff in achieving organizational effectiveness.

3. Specify the basic research funding level needed to implement the recommended agenda for future ARI research.

the committee's final recommendations for a program of basic scientific research on the roles of social and organizational factors as determinants and moderators of the performance of individual soldiers and small units.

The study's statement of task calls for the development of a basic research agenda for ARI, and ARI is the primary intended audience of this report. Through the study process, the committee learned about the experiences of Army soldiers and small units, but the committee did not conduct a scientific assessment of the Army or the military environments in which it operates. However, through its assessment of possible social and organizational factors relevant to Army small units that could be topics of a basic research agenda, the committee expects that the research topics identified in this report are relevant to entities outside the Army that also operate in military environments—to include, for example, other U.S. military services. The committee believes the topics identified for future research will be useful to a broader audience than strictly ARI, and therefore, this report has multiple intended audiences.

Certain important topics were explicitly excluded from the committee's consideration. For example, questions concerning the personnel composition of teams and organizations were not addressed. There is a large literature on this important topic (see, for example, Bell, 2007; Kozlowski and Bell, 2013), but the topic was too close to research on individual differences, which is the focus of another, simultaneous NRC study requested by ARI. The committee was also asked to focus on enduring underlying social and organizational factors relevant across military environments and that likely contribute to many behaviors of interest. For this reason, the report does not analyze or develop a research agenda for specific policies or procedures currently under review by Army leadership (e.g., sexual assault in the military; rate of suicides among active duty soldiers). The committee discussed many of these important behaviors of interest and sought to identify the underlying factors that may be least understood and that, if more fully understood, may have the most promise to make a positive impact on soldiers and small units. This is the basis for many of the topics included in the research agenda presented in this report.

The Current Role of the U.S. Army Research Institute for the Behavioral and Social Sciences

This report outlines the committee's proposed research agenda for ARI's Foundational Science Research Unit,[1] which connects the military and the behavioral and social science research community. This ARI unit is focused on basic research (or "6.1 Basic Research"). As described in an ARI broad agency announcement (U.S. Army Research Institute for the Behavioral and Social Sciences, 2013, p. 3; also see Office of Management and Budget, 2013):

> Basic Research is defined as systematic study directed toward greater knowledge or understanding of the fundamental aspects of phenomena and of observable facts without specific application of processes or products in mind. The ARI's Foundational Science Research Unit manages the Basic Research Program and maintains close contact with ARI's applied scientists and other relevant agencies within the Army. These contacts help define issues that require fundamental research, ensure that the basic research program is coordinated across Services, and facilitate the transition of basic research results to applied programs for eventual use by the operational Army.

A recent ARI special report (2014) lists six research portfolios being supported by ARI: Personnel Testing and Performance, Learning in Formal and Informal Environments, Leader Development, Organizational Effectiveness, Socio-Cultural Capabilities, and Psychophysiology of Individual Differences. This research is conducted through intramural (ARI researchers), extramural (researchers outside ARI to include academia and private entities), and collaborative mechanisms. Currently, ARI provides approximately $6 million in research funds annually to individual projects across its research portfolios.

In addition to its basic research program, ARI also conducts and supports applied research and advanced technology development. A summary of ARI's mission and the importance of its basic research program are provided in Box 1-2. In discussions with ARI through the course of this study, two criteria were emphasized in considering potential projects for ARI's basic research program: (1) the research questions must be grounded in theory, and (2) clear potential must exist to develop the findings of the basic research into an applied research program. In developing the pro-

---

[1]Throughout this report, any reference to ARI is intended to refer to ARI's Foundational Science Research Unit, which manages the basic research portfolio of ARI. It is not the committee's intention to refer to any other units within ARI, specifically those units that manage applied research programs.

Box 1-2

The following is excerpted from a 2013 ARI report, *Foundational Research in the Behavioral and Social Sciences: Marching Towards the Future* (2013b):

> The U.S. Army Research Institute for the Behavioral and Social Sciences (ARI) is the Army's lead agency for the conduct of research and development in the behavioral and social sciences focused on addressing personnel, organization, training, and leader development issues. ARI is a Field Operating Agency of the Office of the Deputy Chief of Staff, G-1, Headquarters, Department of the Army. ARI supports the DCS, G-1 via basic research, applied research, and advanced technology development aimed at improving Army readiness and performance.
>
> The Basic Research program is managed within the Foundational Science Research Unit of ARI, and focuses on creating new knowledge and concepts in support of Army needs, through the conduct of foundational research (6.1) in high-risk, high-reward areas. Broad program goals are searching out and advancing state-of-the-art theory, measures, and methods in the behavioral and social sciences. This includes research that represents paradigm shifts as well as more incremental theory building. The basic research program provides the scientific basis for the Army to modernize the personnel testing, training, and leader development systems of the Army, as well as explore avenues for the Army to maximize unit effectiveness.
>
> The Basic Research program is a critical link between the military and the scientific community within the behavioral and social sciences. ARI's researchers within the basic research program maintain close contact with ARI's applied research units as well as the foundational research organizations within the Department of Defense. This regular communication enables the basic research program to define new issues requiring fundamental research, ensures that the basic research program is coordinated across military services, and facilitates the transition of basic research results to applied research programs for eventual use by the Army.

posed research agenda presented in this report, the committee remained cognizant of the importance of these criteria.

The Bottom Line

Through the course of the committee's deliberations, three key points emerged that are reflected throughout this report. First, the committee is convinced that a basic understanding of soldier and small unit behaviors that are critical for Army success in military environments cannot be suitably conducted wholly outside a military context. It is absolutely essential that basic research programs to understand the unique social and organizational factors that affect soldiers be developed to unify theory and research from academic and laboratory environments with basic research conducted on real soldiers in actual military environments at the small unit level, thereby providing ecological validity of the results. Therefore, ARI's Foundational Science Research Unit should seek opportunities to facilitate basic research conducted in military environments (see Recommendation 1). Second, basic research efforts are needed to develop unit-level measurements of social and organizational factors to enable the Army to better understand the context that influences individual and small unit behavior. Understanding the behavior of small units will contribute to an effective use of units in a leaner force that must achieve missions with optimal efficiency. The potential value of such unit-level measurements is explained in more detail through the recommended research topics (see recommendations included in Chapters 2-6), and the feasibility of such measures is possible through the committee's third and final key point. Third, the committee recommends the development of a new longitudinal survey strategy to track individuals and small units, to include a longitudinal database to retain and maintain administrative and survey data in such a way as to facilitate exploratory research programs reliant upon such data (see Recommendations 7.1, 7.2, and 7.3 in Chapter 7). For the convenience of ARI and other U.S. military funding agencies that may support the basic research called for in this report, Chapter 8 consolidates the committee's conclusions and recommendations into a single location. The committee provides recommendations for a proposed research agenda, but the bottom line of this report lies in the three key points: (1) conduct basic research on soldiers at the small-unit level; (2) develop unit-level measurements of social and organizational factors; and (3) develop a longitudinal survey and maintain a longitudinal database.

Understanding Today's Army

The current Army is composed of almost 1.1 million all-volunteer personnel, about one-half active duty (97,000 officers and 418,000 enlisted soldiers [Army Times, 2014]) and one-half Reserve and National Guard (Department of Defense, 2012; Feickert, 2014). In addition, a civilian workforce of approximately 270,000 personnel directly supports Army operations (McHugh and Odierno, 2013). In 2013, more than 168,000 soldiers were deployed or forward-stationed in 150 countries outside the United States, with active combat operations under way in Afghanistan (McHugh and Odierno, 2013). Impending downsizing directives require that the overall size of the Army will decrease, and while the final numbers remain under review, current guidance will reduce the total Army force to under a million soldiers by the end of 2017 (McHugh and Odierno, 2013; Feickert, 2014).

The Army is large and complex, but it is governed by a distinctively clear collection of rules and regulations, including a code of conduct, a set of seven core values,[2] and mission statements. Larger formations (corps, division, and brigade levels) work in concert to accomplish the larger organizational mission. Although the Army has many well-defined, stable formal structures and regulations, it has been flexible in adapting to dramatic changes in the world in which it operates and in the missions and objectives that guide its operations. Today's Army must succeed in a wider array of missions than ever before while simultaneously adjusting to changing combat and threat deterrent missions and global humanitarian missions. Modern Army units are also much more likely to serve in joint, interagency, intergovernmental, and multinational environments, serving alongside soldiers and commanders from other national or international armies and other military services as well as nongovernmental entities, all of which underscore the importance of cultural understanding and communication skills.

To further complicate the matter, military missions often require rapid decision making and coordination with others in novel ways, so that personnel are not simply following a specific set of tactical orders but are required to understand the broader mission to take initiative to develop and choose among courses of action for successful mission command. Like any workforce, the Army is diverse in terms of demographic characteristics such as gender and race, with increasing pressure to ensure equal opportunities across all demographic groups. Female soldiers currently make up approximately 16 percent of the total Army (Department of Defense, 2012), and the potential effects of the recent shift in policy to review placing female soldiers (i.e., either allowing or requesting an exclusion from placement) into units and positions intended for engagement in direct combat are not yet fully understood. With these challenges and others, many of which are identified and discussed in this report, comes the urgent need to better understand how contextual factors influence soldier and small unit behavior and mission performance.

The formality of the military as an organization, combined with the uniqueness of military environments, fosters the development of a culture in American soldiers distinct from most civilian environments, a culture that is further defined by the Army's specialty branches and a soldier's unit assign-

---

[2]Descriptions of the Seven Core Army Values are available at http://www.army.mil/values/ [April 2014].

ment. From a research standpoint, the uniformity of formal organizational structures and regulations in the Army and the large aggregate of personnel representing diverse backgrounds provide an unparalleled opportunity to conduct innovative scientific studies, breaking new paths for understanding the impact of social and organizational factors on the behaviors of individuals and small units in the context of military environments. The committee believes this opportunity makes the research agenda it proposes here particularly exciting for scientific communities both internal and external to the military.

FRAMEWORK FOR RESEARCH AGENDA

The following sections describe essential elements of the framework for the research agenda recommended in this report, consistent with the study's charge and the committee's assessment of basic research opportunities to further understanding of individual and small unit behavior in military environments.

The Army Small Unit

In accordance with the statement of task, this report focuses on the social and organizational factors that influence individual and small unit behavior. Through the course of this study, the committee made a great effort to understand the importance and dynamics of the Army small unit. Within the Army organizational structure, the term "small unit" is understood to refer to a group of soldiers assigned together as a team, squad, or platoon. Generally speaking, small units are primarily composed of junior enlisted soldiers who are organized into teams and squads (up to 12 enlisted soldiers in a squad), led by a sergeant or staff sergeant, with squads further organized into platoons (up to 4 squads and 50 soldiers in a platoon), each led by a lieutenant.

Through its discussions with military service members and its review of the relevant doctrine and research, the committee concludes that expectations and capabilities of soldiers at the Army small unit level are generally distinct from those of the commissioned officers who lead larger elements (echelons above the platoon). The committee's impression is that the platoon is the Army organizational unit most palpable to the individual enlisted soldier and that the platoon leaders define authority and are the primary source of "orders" for most of these soldiers. We also believe that the "command climate" in a platoon is an essential focus of operational and ethical responsibility when, for example, higher-level leaders want to improve the performance and morale of individual soldiers. To simplify the discussions, unless otherwise noted the primary focus of this report is the generic platoon consisting of three squads. However, it is also important to remember that the idealized platoon to which our discussion typically refers is a paradigm, and reality is much more complicated.

Basic Research on Relevant Personnel

In conducting this study, the committee reviewed a large body of relevant research that contributed to the committee's assessment of future basic research opportunities that should be pursued by ARI. While there are internal Army research programs conducted on soldiers, some of which are noted specifically in this report, the committee is concerned by the limited applicability of many basic research findings that are too far removed from the context of actual soldiers' experiences.

The committee cautions that basic research to understand behavior in military environments cannot be effectively performed on college students and other populations whose contexts are remote from the military environment. Research on contextual factors—such as many of those identified in this report—is not likely to generalize from a controlled research laboratory situation to the situation of interest in actual military environments. Furthermore, using analogues in experimental research may be useful to establish basic effects but needs to be complemented with research in actual military environments. Through the process of this study, the committee became convinced that a significant portion of basic research on the effects of social and organizational factors must be conducted on soldiers in actual military environments. Such research is called "use-inspired basic research" (Stokes, 1997). The challenges and opportunities of military environments can and should inform basic research questions and provide a clear pathway to the future development of applied research programs designed to inform specific policies, procedures, or programs.

To be maximally effective, the committee's proposed research agenda requires that the general mission of ARI's Foundational Science Research Unit should be adjusted so that it serves as a gateway facilitating research, by external (mostly academic) researchers and internal ARI staff researchers, on active duty soldiers in their natural military environments (to include military training or simulated operational environments experienced by small units). This is essential if productive research is to be conducted on the role of contextual factors as determinants of individual and small unit behavior. This led the committee to a single conclusion and its paired recommendation that stand separate from the report's six proposed topical research areas but convey a theme carried through in each of the subsequent conclusions and recommendations.

Conclusion 1
ARI's definition of "basic research" does not preclude scientific research on active duty soldiers in real military contexts. "Basic research is defined as systematic study directed toward fuller knowledge or understanding of the fundamental aspects of phenomena and of observable facts without specific applications towards processes or products in mind" (Office of Management and Budget, 2013, p. 268 [p. 8 of Section 84]).

Recommendation 1
The committee strongly recommends that the Department of the Army support an appropriate mix of intramural and extramural basic scientific research on relevant Army personnel in military environments. The U.S. Army Research Institute for the Behavioral and Social Sciences (ARI) should be responsible for making appropriate data on Army units available and for promoting access for both internal and external behavioral researchers to study basic scientific questions in military contexts. ARI should increase its role as a facilitator or gateway for basic behavioral research in military contexts.

The committee recognizes that soldiers have critical jobs to perform and their time is valuable; they are not an unlimited research subject pool. Furthermore, concerns about confidentiality, privacy, and internal review boards will need to be addressed. And access to soldiers across environments, including in garrison and training as well as environments where mortality salience adds a critically important dimension, will pose challenges to implementation. However, the committee is firmly resolved that, from a basic research perspective, the payoff in understanding real soldiers in real military environments far outweighs the effort that may be necessary to conduct the research. Furthermore, the committee believes ARI is well positioned to serve as a key connection between researchers and soldiers—conveying to researchers the challenges and opportunities faced by troops and conveying to soldiers the value of scientific research targeting those challenges and opportunities and facilitating access to soldiers for research purposes. And the committee encourages ARI to seek creative ideas to gain access to soldiers in efficient ways, such as potentially leveraging junior and senior officers assigned to the academic faculty of military academies, to include senior faculty who have regular short-term rotations into operational units.

Social and Organizational Factors in the Context of Military Environments

One of the major challenges for the committee in answering its charge was to reach consensus on how to "identify key contextual factors that shape individual and small unit behavior" (see subtask 1 in Box 1-1). Early in the study process, the committee considered many potentially relevant contextual factors, for example: small unit dynamics in which individuals work; organizational factors that define and constrain approaches to performance; societal factors such as the media, public opinion, or remote communications with family; organizational moral-ethical climate; physical structure, technology, and environment surrounding the unit; mix of family, ethnic, and cultural history in the unit; a soldier's family and social networks; nature and severity of external threats and disruptions to the unit; performance evaluation of individual unit members; the extent and nature of training and experiences shared; and generational gaps and differences in behavioral and social characteristics. During the study's data-gathering sessions, which included formal briefings and prepared papers as well as informal panel discussions with active and recently separated Army soldiers, the committee considered many more social and organizational factors that may be relevant to individual and small unit behavior in military environments. The committee understands that within small units, behaviors are dynamic, changing sequences of actions among individuals who, in turn, may modify their actions and reactions partly as a function of the actions and reactions of other unit members. Moreover, these interactions reflect a wide range of factors that ultimately influence them.

After an initial discussion, the committee decided not to attempt to develop a more precise concept of "key contextual factors" or to reach consensus on precisely how to delineate this complex concept. We did not use the concept to define limits or to constrain the research proposals created in response to the statement of task. Instead various threads of the concept were simply used as "jumping off" points to support directed but divergent lines of thought.

As the reader moves to the body of the report where the committee provides details of the contextual factors recommended for future research, an important general point to keep in mind is that there are many "key contextual factors" in military environments. The factors on which this report focuses emerged through committee deliberations as especially relevant, in the committee's expert opinion, to increase basic knowledge of the social and organizational factors that influence soldiers and small units in military environments. In selecting those factors presented in this report, the committee carefully considered the quality and extent of existing research, largely conducted in academic settings, as well as applicable research that may have been conducted within military environments. Several opportunities to converse with soldiers afforded the committee insight into the experiences of Army small units in tactical military environments; however, the committee recognizes that the Army is an organization and any given soldier's experiences within that organization are far more complex than what could be learned in the short time of this study or what could be conveyed in this report. The committee's discussions with Army soldiers facilitated committee deliberations on the hypothesized applicability of findings developed from existing, primarily academic, research to Army soldiers and on the potential benefit of future research to develop better understanding of Army soldiers and the uniqueness of the environments in which they operate. This study was not intended to understand all factors that shape Army small unit behavior, and the social and organizational factors presented here are not the only relevant contextual factors. Instead, this report presents opportunities for future research based on the committee's judgment of the most promising areas to pursue given prior research findings, basic theory, and factors of apparent key relevance to military environments. Understanding these factors—as well as others that may take on added importance as the world, and the Army's role within it, continues to shift—will be important for the future of the Army. As it proved for many members of the committee, Figure 1-1 may be a useful mnemonic or conceptual framework for readers to visualize the interactions between contextual factors and individual and unit behavior that ultimately determine small unit performance. This is the perspective from which the committee presents a proposed research agenda, which is to be implemented through access to real soldiers in real environments and with a coherent long-term funding strategy (see following section).

Effective Research Funding Strategies

The statement of task requires the committee to comment on the level of funding necessary to implement the recommended research agenda. We find it impossible to provide specific numbers, in part because our review of the records and mission statements we have been able to obtain describing Department of Defense, Army, and ARI budgets has left us confused as to the rationales for allocating funds among various funding categories. The committee was not provided with the resources or the data to conduct a full financial analysis necessary to offer detailed cost estimates of the proposed research agenda or to assess the necessary funds against ARI's current funding levels or projects. Furthermore, it was outside the scope of this committee's tasks to conduct the more thorough project design required to develop more accurate cost estimates. Instead, the committee made a good faith estimation of appropriate funding levels, based on the

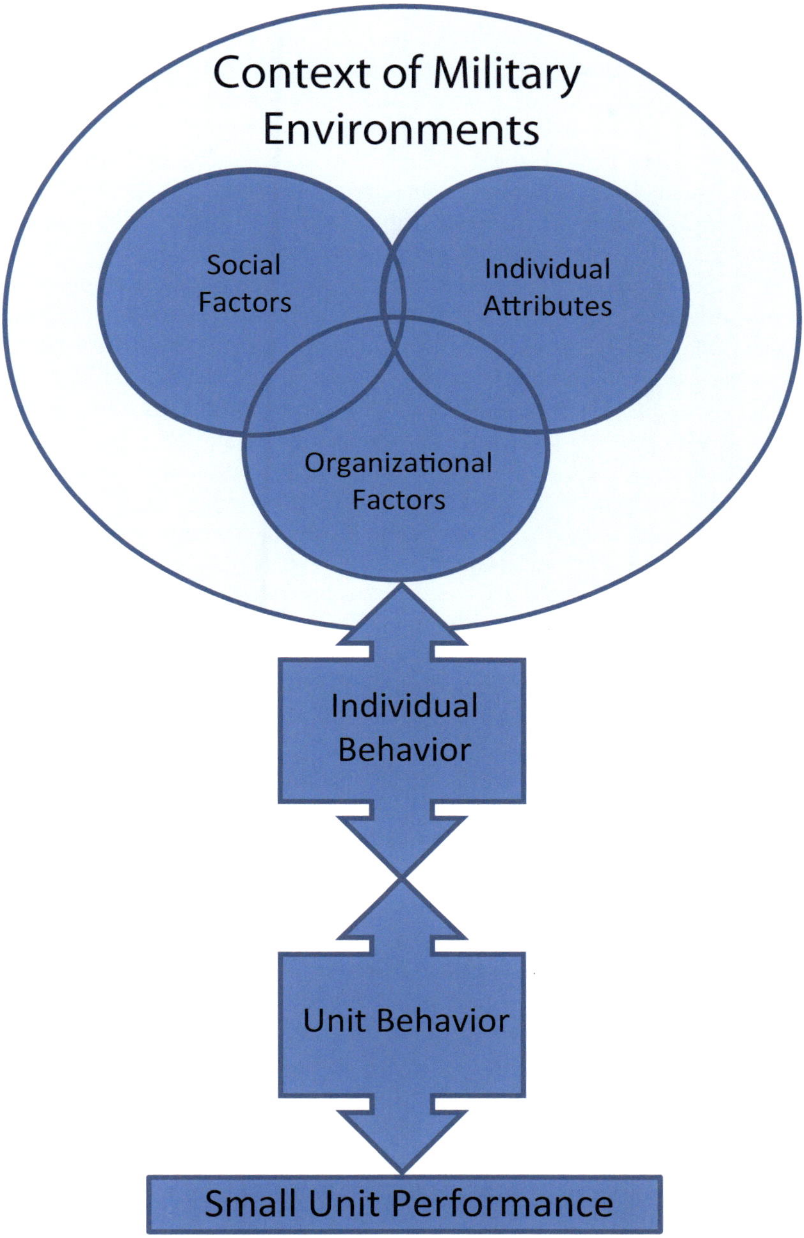

FIGURE 1-1 Context of military environments: interactions between contextual factors and behaviors that contribute to small unit performance.

members' own personal experiences as academic researchers. In any case, the following remarks are offered to assist the Assistant Secretary of the Army for Acquisition, Logistics, and Technology when considering research funding strategies for ARI basic research over the next 10 or more years. These remarks are not intended to provide funding justification for specific research programs, but their value is in highlighting important considerations to develop a cohesive and effective research strategy to develop fundamental knowledge in areas the committee judges to have enduring importance to the Army across military environments.

First, it would be unproductive to make small allocations of funds across several of the initiatives featured in the committee's research recommendations. Funds should be allocated to develop high-quality programs (with high impact potential for the Army), in small numbers if necessary due to limited funds, rather than to develop a large number of programs with breadth but without sufficient depth. If limitations on funds constrain resourcing the entire recommended research agenda, then ARI should choose one or more of the initiatives and fund several complementary projects within each chosen initiative that are likely to reinforce one another and result in a substantial contribution. Two factors ARI could consider in prioritizing focal areas are the direct relevance of the Army context and the likelihood that this research would be carried out by other entities if the Army does not fund it. To use limited resources most efficiently, areas central and unique to the Army context and areas of inquiry that are not likely to be funded elsewhere or conducted without funding would therefore be given priority.

Second, suppose that funds were only available to support one of the topical initiatives in the proposed research agenda. To be effective, the committee believes that funds should be allocated to a small number of high-quality projects focused on that initiative, running concurrently and ideally with complementary research plans, with an appropriate multiyear minimum-duration commitment to allow the projects to be fully developed and refined. For example, suppose three projects were funded to study the development and effects of norms in military contexts. We could imagine one project based on interviews and embedded observers, another based on tracking interaction patterns with unobtrusive electronic signaling devices (worn on their uniforms, with the participants' knowledge and consent), and a third based on experiments to test soldiers' and their leaders' behaviors and decision making when they encounter new situations. Ideally these studies would be conducted with consenting soldiers during training, deployment, or garrison assignments over multiple years, recognizing the potential impact on research data collected on soldiers whose experiences rotate through the Army Force Generation 3-year cycle (Department of the Army, 2011).

The committee was unable to assess precisely a total cost for such a project, because we do not know how the Army would account for participant costs when the participants are active duty soldiers. But, the expected research expenses would be comparable to current ARI funding levels per project, with the addition of funds for participant support and investigator travel to Army locations to conduct the research. Furthermore, beyond initial projects suggested to last at least 3 years, for the research to make a substantial contribution, the initiative would need a continuing commitment of 6-10 years (permitting critical longitudinal data collection on participating soldiers as they complete two or more iterations of the current Army Force Generation's 3-year cycle) to allow the first projects to be suitably conducted and analyzed and for further research to be refined and expanded based upon the preliminary studies.

Third, the committee's support for the proposed longitudinal survey project (see Chapter 7) is based on the survey's likely contribution in advancing basic scientific objectives in understanding human behavior in organizations with distinctive cultures, like that of the Army. This understanding provides a background, big picture context for some of the other recommended research initiatives described in Chapters 2-6. The survey would provide concrete, factual information that would directly inform and guide Army policies concerning, for example, women's careers in the military, the occurrence of troublesome behaviors of interest in various military settings, and early warnings of potential shortages in personnel capabilities as the Army's missions change with the changing world situation. We were unable to obtain useful data concerning the costs of comparable studies such as the Millennium Cohort Study, but we suggest that, if policy makers decide to initiate the survey, the Millennium Cohort Study budget could be reviewed for information useful in estimating costs.

To use the resulting database for exploratory studies, the longitudinal survey project will need to include funds to attract researchers internal and external to ARI. This funding would be additional, beyond the funding required for the data collection and database construction and maintenance.

The committee encourages the Army to allocate funds sufficient to support at least several of the research programs proposed in this report. Although we cannot estimate the funding level required in exact dollar amounts, we can say that, to effectively implement the proposed research agenda without decrement to existing programs of research, the ARI budget would need to increase to levels of "double digit" millions of dollars per year.

The basic research program proposed in this report is intended to advance understanding of fundamental behavioral phenomena. It is designed to be innovative, and it requires consequential changes from current ARI policies and practices. It is intensely focused on understanding the behavior of real soldiers in real military environments. Furthermore, the questions at which the various initiatives are directed are descriptive and practical, with potential to be developed into applied research programs. They are grounded in theory but are not motivated solely by intangible theoretical concerns. The studies the committee proposes for funding are intended to be directly useful to Army policy makers as they further basic understanding of behavioral and social problems and opportunities in the next decade and beyond of Army missions.

REPORT OUTLINE

The body of this report includes six chapters, each developing specific proposals for research. Each chapter provides (1) a review of relevant scientific findings, theories, and perspectives that led the committee to judge the topic as particularly relevant for further basic research, especially to be conducted on soldiers in military environments; and (2) illustrative examples of pertinent scientific questions and suggestions for concrete research directions. Between the topics proposed for future research, the committee found significant variations in the extent to which the topic has been previously studied inside and outside military settings, and the contents of the chapters reflect these variations (e.g., Army doctrine has long emphasized the importance of leadership, whereas the committee could only generalize academic research on environmental transitions that suggests relevance to the experiences of soldiers and small units). The chapters also include recommendations for basic research programs that could be developed as requests for proposals for funding by ARI or other U.S. military funding agencies.

In Chapters 2 through 6, the committee presents its assessments and recommendations for future research on five key types of social and organizational factors that warrant study at the unit level of measurement: norms, environmental transitions, power and status, contextual leadership, and multiteam systems. Chapter 7 addresses the collection of longitudinal survey data on those topics that the committee judges to be the most promising to maximize organizational effectiveness within the U.S. Army. Chapter 7 also calls for the development of a longitudinal database to collect administrative and survey data to facilitate exploratory research programs reliant upon such data. Finally, for the convenience of ARI and other U.S. military funding agencies that may implement basic research programs on the topics proposed in this report, Chapter 8 provides a consolidated list of the committee's conclusions and recommendations.

REFERENCES

Army Times. (2014). 10K soldiers must go this year, 20K next year. May 12. Available: http://www.armytimes.com/article/20140512/CAREERS/305120014/ [May 2014].

Bell, S.T. (2007). Deep-level composition variables as predictors of team performance: A meta-analysis. *Journal of Applied Psychology,* 92(3):595-615.

Department of the Army. (2011). *Military Operations: Army Force Generation.* Army Regulation 525-29. Washington, DC: Headquarters, Department of the Army. Available: http://www.forscom.army.mil/graphics/r525_29.pdf [June 2014].

Department of Defense. (2012). *2012 Demographics: Profile of the Military Community.* Office of the Deputy Assistant Secretary of Defense (Military Community and Family Policy). Available: http://www.armyg1.army.mil/hr/docs/demographics/FY12_ARMY_PROFILE.pdf [June 2014].

Feickert, A. (2014). *Army Drawdown and Restructuring: Background and Issues for Congress.* CRS Report 7-5700. Washington, DC: Congressional Research Service. Available: http://www.fas.org/sgp/crs/natsec/R42493.pdf [April 2014].

Kozlowski, S.W.J., and B.S. Bell. (2013). Work groups and teams in organizations. In Randy K. Otto, Ed., *Handbook of Psychology,* 2nd ed., Vol. 12 (pp. 412-469). New York: Wiley.

McHugh, J.M., and R.T. Odierno. (2013). Statement before the Committee on Armed Services, United States Senate First Session, 113th Congress, on the Posture of the United States Army. April 23. Available: http://www.armed-services.senate.gov/imo/media/doc/McHugh-Odierno_04-23-13(1).pdf [April 2014].

National Research Council. (2008). *Human Behavior in Military Contexts.* Committee on Opportunities in Basic Research in the Behavioral and Social Sciences for the U.S. Military. James J. Blascovich and Christine R. Hartel, Eds., Board on Behavioral, Cognitive, and Sensory Sciences, Division of Behavioral and Social Sciences and Education. Washington, DC: The National Academies Press.

Office of Management and Budget. (2013). Circular No. A-11 Preparation, Submission, and Execution of the Budget. Executive Office of the President, July 2013. Available: http://www.whitehouse.gov/sites/default/files/omb/assets/a11_current_year/a11_2013.pdf [April 2014].

Stokes, D.E. (1997). *Pasteur's Quadrant, Basic Science and Technological Innovation.* Washington, DC: Brookings Institution Press.

U.S. Army Research Institute for the Behavioral and Social Sciences. (2013). *Improvement of Army Readiness and Performance via Research Advances and Applications of the Behavioral and Social Sciences (Personnel, Organization, Training, and Leader Development Issues).* Solicitation Number W911NF-13-R-0001. ARI FY 13-18 Broad Agency Announcement. Available: https://www.fbo.gov/?s=opportunity&mode=form&id=102faad5082fa9d2881ec483fe166c2b&tab=core&_cview=1 [April 2014].

U.S. Army Research Institute for the Behavioral and Social Sciences. (2014). *Foundational Research in Behavioral and Social Sciences: Marching Towards the Future. Special Report No. 73.* Washington, DC: Department of the Army.

2

Norms in Military Environments

"Norms are cultural phenomena that prescribe and proscribe behavior in specific circumstances" (Hechter and Opp, 2001, p. xi). They are group-level phenomena that guide how people behave, or believe they should behave, in groups (*injunctive* norms; described in more detail below). Norms also refer to group perceptions about behavior, irrespective of morality or compatibility with social or organizational values or ethics (*descriptive* norms; described in more detail below). Research questions concerning norms and how they operate in military contexts can address a broad cross-section of topics and issues; for instance:

- In novel contexts or settings, how do norms emerge within Army units?
- How do soldiers respond to Army policy that seeks to change norms, as well as how norms change on their own accord?
- What causes individuals to deviate from sanctioned institutional norms? What causes groups of individuals to subscribe to norms that deviate from institutional values?
- How do soldiers formally and informally sanction the non-normative or deviant behavior of their peers?
- How do soldiers successfully negotiate the translation of Army core values into normative behavior?
- How do norms become disconnected from Army core values?
- What social norms predict Army unit success?
- How does the acute and chronic stress that many Army units experience influence the above?

PERSPECTIVES ON NORMS RESEARCH

Although the concept of norms is one of the most common concepts used by social scientists to explain behavior (Sills and Merton, 1968), the definition of norms, how they emerge, how they operate, why people comply with them, and the influence of sanctioning on compliance remain controversial. Complicating these matters, academic disciplines discuss norms using different terminology and constructs (e.g., anthropologists discuss "cultural norms;" economists discuss profit maximization and self-interested behavior in terms of "expected utility" and "Nash equilibrium") and research them using a variety of methods (e.g., ethnography, survey methods, laboratory experiments, computer simulation). Nevertheless, it is generally accepted that social norms are an essential feature of all human groups.

Through its review of the available research, the committee recognizes the potential to develop a far more detailed and lengthy chapter discussing distinct concepts of norms and their potential relevance to military environments. However, the committee had two specific intentions in authoring this chapter: (1) to introduce the U.S. Army Research Institute for the Behavioral and Social Sciences and other research agencies to the substantial academic work on norms that has been conducted outside the context of military environments, and (2) to suggest key basic research opportunities that have great potential to improve understanding of real soldiers operating in real military environments. The perspectives on norms research offered in this section introduce the complexity of the study of norms. While this section will define and distinguish types of norms that operate through different mechanisms, for the purposes of the research agenda recommended in this report, such differences between norms is of less consequence. The committee assesses that understanding norms in military environments is important, and should be considered for future research without stipulating detail that might otherwise obscure the broad-spectrum importance of norms as a contextual influence on soldiers and small units. In this way the committee supports norms research without specifically directing or shaping that agenda to one type of norms research.

Norms are understood in terms of two distinguishable characteristics that often combine in how group and individual members behave and perceive behavior, according to the norm. On one hand, norms refer to the "oughtness" of behavior (Homans, 1950), highlighting the moral sentiment group members have about what "should" and "should not" happen (Hechter and Opp, 2001). These *injunctive* norms (Cialdini et al., 1990) reflect group assessment of "approved" and "disapproved" conduct. In this regard, norms signify values or the shared belief system of a group. On the other hand, norms reference behaviors and beliefs held in common by group members regardless of morality, defined as *descriptive* norms. This "normative" behavior allows members to conform to other members of the group (Cialdini, 1988), as well as providing expectations concerning how other members will behave (Bicchieri, 2006). Descriptive norms are common behaviors or how most people in a group act, or are anticipated to act, in specific situations.

Although many aspects of norms are contested across disciplines, much of the research validates a long-standing hypothesis that norms will emerge to solve collective action problems (Ullman-Margalit, 1977). However, this is not the only condition under which norms form, nor does it assume norms are always positive; for example, they may have disadvantages for some members (Opp, 2001). Furthermore, injunctive norms can emerge through ". . . the aggregate results of human action with no thought or no intention of bringing about a norm" (Opp, 2001, p. 237).

Research on social norms typically emphasizes the interrelated process of compliance and sanctioning. It is implicit in the concept of norms that in most instances people comply with them (Cialdini et al., 1988). Similarly, if group members disobey an injunctive norm, members may sanction one another, i.e., the majority may engage in efforts to "correct" the behaviors of minority group members (Heckathorn, 1990). However, when the majority of group members disobey injunctive norms, deviating group members may not sanction the majority (Cialdini, 1988); in these cases, descriptive norms outweigh injunctive norms. While this generic understanding of social norms is relatively undisputed, theoretical explanations concerning their importance, as well as how they operate, remain controversial topics (see Keizer et al., 2008, for an example of a study of behavioral effects when descriptive and injunctive norms are in conflict).

Theories of the formation of norms and the effectiveness of norms have been developed by many researchers, including anthropologists, sociologists, economists, historians, and psychologists, and these theories often have somewhat different focus and different implications for addressing deviant behavior. Several theories have been influential in sociology. Parsons' (1951) theory of the socialized actor argues that self-interested individuals voluntarily conform to social norms because these norms become part of the personality of the individual. Parsons does not provide a theory of how norms are formed but rather views norms as exogenous. They are internally enforced by feelings of shame or guilt, are primarily taught by parents, and so become part of the preferences of individuals. In this way, norms become values. The implications of the theory of the socialized actor are that norms will change only slowly and that norms predict behavior.

Yet, there are many examples of an individual's norms changing rapidly, such as when an individual decides to join a new group (such as the Army) and wants to be accepted as part of that group. Moreover, some research suggests that injunctive norms often do not predict behavior unless the individual believes that others will behave in accordance with a particular norm (Ajzen and Fishbein, 1980; Fishbein and Ajzen, 1977, 1975). In other words, contrary to Parsons' theory, compliance with norms is not unconditional. Rather, people often comply with norms because of what that compliance implies about their group membership and consequent self-image. For example, social identity theory (Tajfel, 1981; Turner et al., 1987) notes that by choosing to join a particular group, the individual redefines his or her self-image in ways that are congruent with the roles, beliefs, values, and actions of the group. This could be particularly relevant for soldiers as they join specialty branches of the Army (e.g., infantry or intelligence) or divisions with well-known distinguished histories (e.g., 10th Mountain Division or 82nd Airborne Division). In essence, by joining a group, an individual internalizes a self-image that is consistent with any stereotypic image of, or scripted behavior associated with, the group.

Rational Choice and the Effectiveness of Norms

There are three mechanisms through which norms can be enforced, thereby making them effective at influencing group behavior. First, a rational self-interested individual will conform to a norm if the expected sanctions are sufficient (Axelrod, 1986; Coleman, 1990; Bendor and Swistak, 2001). In this case, compliance with social norms can be analyzed in terms of the formal game theory construct called a "repeated prisoner's dilemma."

A second mechanism is the internalization of norms (i.e., self-discipline): for example, an individual might not litter, even if no one else sees, because the individual will feel guilty for behaving in an "immoral" manner (Cialdini and Trost, 1998). For an internalized norm, external enforcement through mechanisms such as fines is unnecessary; the norm has become part of the individual's preferences. The example of littering illustrates one economic role of social norms: to improve efficiency by removing externalities. However, the real question is whether and how norms can evolve without sanctions (e.g., fines for littering) or internalization (e.g., respect for the environment).

In a third mechanism, norms develop based on the expectations of how others will behave (Bicchieri, 2006), which implies conditional conformity if it becomes in the self-interest of all or most participants to conform (i.e., a stable Nash equilibrium). For example, should one decide to drive on the right or left side of the road (Young, 1996)? Applying this third mechanism, the answer depends on the individual's expectation of what others will do. In this example, the norm is enforced by the desire to prevent accidents (a coordination motive). Coordination games that evolve an efficient, stable social norm as an equilibrium (from possible multiple equilibria, e.g., either driving on the left or driving on the right side of the road) provide a clear theory of the formation of a social norm.

Decision Making as a Dual Process

Both to explain deviant behavior and to suggest research avenues for correcting or preventing such behavior, it is useful to review a commonly invoked framework from cognitive psychology for how people make decisions as a dual process (see, for example, Epstein, 1990; Evans, 2007, 2008, 2010; Kahneman and Frederick, 2005; Sloman, 1996; Stanovich, 1999; Chaiken and Trope, 1999). Dual process theories propose that people have two information processing systems that work together to produce judgments and hence behavior: (1) the deliberative reasoning brain and (2) the intuitive and emotional brain, which is often subconscious. Although this framework may be an oversimplification of complex decision making, and there is debate as to whether people harbor two different parallel processing architectures (Evans, 2010, 2012; Sloman, 1996) or merely two different cognitive modes (Kahneman and Frederick, 2005; Stanovich, 1999), many people find the framework useful for explaining behavior. Kahneman has recently summarized much of the extant research in *Thinking Fast and Slow* (2012).

Fast thinking comes from what psychologists call System 1, which influences decisions through immediate feelings that arise in response to a situation or stimulus. These reactions are partly instinctual, partly learned, and often emotional. Slow thinking takes place in System 2, which behaves much like the rational choice or expected utility model of economic theory. Dual process theory holds that decisions typically result from a mix of influences from these two systems. Sometimes System 1 dominates, as when an instant and instinctual response is required in swerving a Humvee to avoid a possible improvised explosive device. At other times, System 2 dominates; for example, when an individual decides between alternative routes to travel to a distant village by taking time to reflect on the relative risks of each possible route.

One of the interesting things about System 1 is that probabilities seem to be ignored in these automated, reflexive, responses that are based on instinct or past learning. System 1 is also activated by change or deviation from a reference point (what is normal or expected), so it is relative and reacts to changes, as opposed to System 2, which considers absolutes. Kahneman (2012) argues that the nervous system is very sensitive to changes from reference points and codes changes as positive (pleasure) or negative (pain). Many studies have shown that losses from a reference point seem to be valued about twice as much as gains and that people generally prefer to avoid losses than to acquire gains; they are typically risk-seeking in losses (e.g., prefer a 50-50 percent risk of no loss or a $2,500 loss rather than to accept a certain $1,000 loss) and risk-averse in gains (e.g., prefer to receive a certain $1,000 than a 50-50 percent chance of gaining $2,500 or gaining nothing), features that have their origin in System 1 (Kahneman and Tversky, 1984). Understanding the role of System 1 in decisions made by soldiers, who may generally be more risk-seeking individuals than the typical populations used for such studies, may have important implications for understanding how norms develop in small units.

When System 1 and System 2 are in conflict, context is thought to determine which system dominates. For example, fatigue, stress, or other forms of cognitive load reduce the influence of System 2 (which is the source of rational decision making and self-control) and increase the influence of System 1, leading to more instinctive, habitual, or "mindless" (not consciously reflective) behavior (Shiv and Fedorikhin, 1999). For example, in a study examining the role of dual process in moral decision making, cognitive load was shown to interfere with utilitarian moral judgment, leading subjects to make less deliberative and more emotion-based moral judgments (Greene et al., 2008). An example of this type of decision might occur when soldiers on an infiltration mission come across civilians on the way to their target. Their leader might consider several options in order to accomplish the mission and follow the Law of Land Warfare which prohibits the deliberate killing or wounding of civilians. The existence of clear policy reinforced through training is intended to relieve leaders of having to make deliberative decisions because they are trained to have the correct response. In other words the correct response becomes a reference point in System 1, rather than having to rely on the slower, easily overloaded System 2.

Similarly, in another series of psychology experiments, student subjects placed under cognitive load were much more likely to violate social norms than those who were not (Gailliot et al., 2012). The results suggest that some individuals possess more self-control as an inherent trait and that self-control can be depleted if participants are put under cognitive load. In six experiments, social norms that were either implicit (e.g., do not use curse words) or explicit (e.g., a stated rule of no talking) were consistently more likely to be violated by those participants with low self-control as a trait (measured by a self-report survey) or by participants subjected to self-control depletion by a lengthy, boring task such as crossing out specified letters in written text. These experiments suggest that problem behaviors are more likely to occur when individuals are put under stress. For soldiers, stress could be induced from many sources: combat exposure, personal issues, frequent contact with family at home during deployment, or other sources including too much free time. However, the committee cautions against inferring too much from studies conducted in settings outside military environments which do not properly account for the circumstances experienced by soldiers.

To illustrate the relevance of the dual process typology for understanding norm violation, consider a soldier who is mentally exhausted from combat, inebriated, or troubled by events at home. These cognitive loads may compromise System 2 to the point that if the soldier experiences a severe loss in System 1 (e.g., from an unexpected event), the soldier may not make rationally correct choices and may become angry or risk-seeking. Social norms establish reference points that are learned and are consistent with the concept of *gist,* fuzzy memory representations of the meaning of a past event (Brainerd and Reyna, 1990; Reyna, 2004). Complex information is reduced to simplified rules when learned and encoded in System 1. The advantage of the *gist* of social norms, if they are sufficiently strongly ingrained, is that they can guide behavior without invoking System 2 in cases where System 2 is compromised. Creating such strong norms in a military situation requires extensive learning from training, such as the training soldiers receive on the Seven Core Army Values (loyalty, duty, respect, selfless service, honor, integrity, and personal courage).[1] For example, behavioral problems "behind the wire" may arise if soldiers are extensively trained and have the correct gist for behavior outside of the wire (e.g., protocols for combat engagement with civilians present), but do not receive enough training to develop the correct gist for behavior inside the wire (e.g., treatment of detainees).

An example of reference point formation by System 1 is learning to drive a car. One reference point that needs to be developed is keeping the car in the middle of the lane. If the car drifts left or right, when one is learning to drive, the driver consciously has to think to turn the wheel to the right or left. However this process becomes subconscious and automatic for experienced drivers—unless they fail to pay attention and hear the rumble of the Botts' dots at the side of the road, which evokes an upsetting or fear response and immediate correction (Schulze et al., 2013; see also Martens and Fox, 2007). Reference points can thus be viewed as "automating" behavior or creating habits so that System 2 can be freed to think of more important things. However, reference points can also lead to decision errors.

Norms guide behavior as internalized standards that operate at both the conscious (System 2) and subconscious (System 1) levels. Norm violation can occur when System 2 is compromised (through stress or fatigue), and the System 1 response is counternormative. Some (descriptive) norms are useful for coordinating action; other (injunctive) norms are useful

[1]Descriptions of the Seven Core Army Values are available at http://www.army.mil/values/ [April 2014].

because they instantiate values and reinforce people's self-identity. Given these functions, norms are critical for understanding Army behavior, particularly in small unit settings and when formal rules may be less evident or difficult for soldiers to interpret given the context of the military environment and mission.

CHARACTERISTICS OF NORMS IN ARMY CONTEXTS

Norms concern how a social group patterns its behavior relative to situations (i.e., contexts) its members encounter. As a result, understanding social norms in the Army requires considering the real-world contexts soldiers experience. The following examples demonstrate how norms, or features of them, influence or may potentially influence the behaviors and beliefs of soldiers.

1. *When norms of a group change, the change influences what current, former, or future members of the group think about themselves.*

Policies concerning women in the Army have changed; the new norm allows women to take a greater role in combat operations. Across the "total institution" (Goffman, 1961), Army leadership can change norms, but such changes often encounter resistance. This can be understood in terms of norms as they may follow or precede formal changes to rules or laws. For example, moving from all-male combat units to units that include men and women influences norms soldiers may resent or resist. In this instance, a wide range of previously normative behavior might be affected. As the military is already beginning to recognize, behaviors that would be considered normative within all-male units, such as teasing, insults, or sexual joking or talk, take on new meaning when they occur within mixed-gender units (Wong, 2014). These behaviors, which the group may have previously associated with group bonding, must now be reevaluated for acceptability. Changes (or lack of change) in this regard may also complicate how women soldiers perceive their membership in these units, as well as how they are perceived by others (see Chapter 5). Understanding how soldiers learn acceptable behavior when what "acceptable" means is changing or still being determined (or contested) by the group is a critical research question. Mixed in with this norm are laws regarding "sexual harassment." However, what is legally prohibited and what is socially acceptable (i.e., the norm) are often different, and the line here can be fuzzy. How new norms associated with women in the Army are communicated and negotiated among unit group members—and the larger Army—is critical to consider. The evolving norms associated with women are also particularly meaningful to the Army's effort to recruit women. It should be noted that resisting the norm in this instance is a byproduct of the groups' perceptions and does not have to be based on fact. Furthermore, it was clear to the committee through discussions with military service members that norms are already developing within the military absent official policy, for example in regards to fitness requirements for female soldiers in combat units.

A study of sexual harassment norms in the military, conducted via a cross-sectional survey of 681 active duty soldiers, found harassment-tolerant norms emanating from the soldiers' unit and immediate supervisors but not from senior officers (Murdoch et al., 2009). Several features of military microclimates were suggested to explain these findings. First, because of the hierarchical structure of the military, interactions between senior officers and lower ranks (to include junior officers and enlisted ranks) are limited (Hoffman, 1995). Therefore, norms accepted or promulgated from above may not diffuse to all levels of the military. Second, intra-unit cohesion might influence individual behaviors more than organizational policy. In other words, soldiers feel more loyalty and accountability to other members of their units than to outsiders. From this kind of evidence, the committee judges that results from nonmilitary research, which concludes that management shapes norms more than peer coworkers (Wimbush and Shepard, 1994), may not apply to military small units, where the platoon leader and noncommissioned officers within the platoon have more effect on group norms than do commissioned officers at higher echelons. Although more research needs to be done in this area within military environments, the laboratory-based norms research suggests that norms in small units are not always the product of formal leadership processes.

In game theory and experimental studies of norms, metanorms are defined as mechanisms associated with the enforcement of norms (Axelrod, 1986). In her presentation of a *relational theory of norm enforcement*, Horne (2009) describes compelling experimental and case study evidence concerning how relationships between group members promote metanorms. Simply stated, this theory holds that the more group members are interdependent, the more they will sanction behavior; "their dependence on others can lead them to enforce norms they do not prefer and in which they do not believe" (Horne, 2009, pp. 27-28).

2. *Norms define the expectations that others have of one's behavior as a member of the group.*

Soldiers in the Army "follow orders," but through discussions with military service members, the committee learned that even this most fundamental edict can challenge social norms. For instance, in operations "outside the wire" a squad leader on combat missions has enormous responsibility; as the leader, he or she must make many tactical decisions independently, based on his or her understanding of commander's intent, and these decisions could have strategic implications for the mission and mortality implications for the leader and the unit. However, in garrison, expectations change dramatically; the same squad leader may feel like just another soldier who must follow orders (whatever they may be), adhere to rules, and follow a strict chain of command under centralized leadership.

These shifts in expectations influence norms. Namely, the norms in the former context support values of autonomy, responsibility, independent situational decision making, innovation, and trust, while the norm expectation in the latter context (in garrison) supports values of conformity, rule following, deference, and obedience. Instances in which a change in context exposes contrasting expectations of the group (i.e., "outside the wire you have to be an independent tactical decision maker, inside the wire you have to follow the rules") are important to understanding norm development and conflicts (see also Chapter 3). This example does not imply that rules do not apply "outside the wire." Rather, it is the contrast in expectations guiding the soldiers' behavior (that is, different norms being applied) that complicates matters and makes researching normative processes critical.

3. *What is normative in one social context is deviant in another.*

To a soldier, killing the enemy is normative and conforms to the primary strategic mission of the military. Of course, killing in other contexts (i.e., civilian society) is deviant. But killing may also occur in less clearly defined contexts such as a noncombat operation or when the mission objective is complicated, multidimensional, or insufficiently or inaccurately understood. In these contexts, killing may be considered deviant, in violation of the rules of engagement, or illegal, but its effect on small unit norms can be unpredictable. For whatever reason, members of the unit may believe the act was necessary, warranted, or acceptable. In such instances norms associated with killing can potentially change to accommodate a new context (e.g., a noncombat operation), especially if its ultimate outcome supports values that the group holds (e.g., protecting their peers). These behaviors may, in turn, act to modify the "values" of the unit, or shift unit norms. Although killing is an extreme example, other deviant behaviors may emerge as a function of shifting norms. In this way, systematic norms research in the context of small military units can make important contributions to the understanding of conditional factors and qualities of norms. For instance, in the 2003-2004 Abu Ghraib Detention Facility detainee abuse incidents, norms adopted by a unit (military police) shifted to a point where the treatment of detainees manifested the antithesis of Army core values (see Willer et al., 2009, for a discussion of norms that people compel each other to do but that the group members disapprove of privately). Here again, although norms may be only part of the larger historical context associated with Abu Ghraib, a better understanding of norms can inform developing measures that prevent such deviance. As intense stress can elicit deviant behaviors that may be perceived by groups as normal, understanding norm formation processes is critical to the mission of the Army.

4. *Norms align how people within a social group act toward people in other social groups.*

On the modern battlefield, members of an Army unit are under unique stress because the "others" they encounter may be friend one day and foe the next (see also Chapter 3). Modern warfare requires soldiers to fight enemies who hide among noncombatants, making the rules of engagement, and the legal actions they incur when violated, complex to interpret (Puckett and Atwood, 2012). Confusion is further compounded by the diversity of groups with which the Army collaborates. Here the expectation (i.e., norm) is caution: if it is unclear whether the "others" are allies, then it is best to treat them as a potential enemy to ensure self- and collective force protection. But ironically, behaviors that support this norm may work against its ultimate purpose. Treating a noncombatant as a potential enemy is not a functional way to enlist or maintain that noncombatant as an ally. This context can, in turn, undermine and disrupt mission-related objectives because, in the mind of the soldier, behaviors are associated with different norms. Here, as in the case of sexual harassment, actions can blur the line between normative, deviant, and criminal behavior.

An important objective of the Army is to promote small unit cohesion and other forms of teamwork. But as in the civilian justice system, within military justice the culpability for any collective battlefield crime (e.g., crimes committed by a group of soldiers) falls on the individual soldiers, the soldiers' immediate supervisor, and commanding junior officers (Puckett and Atwood, 2012). Current theories used to understand such crime are very limited, the most notable being "groupthink," which postulates that faulty decisions occur though premature consensus that subverts normal processes (Janis, 1972). Although the groupthink hypothesis, when subjected to experimental tests, has not consistently produced the predicted results (Moorhead, 1982; Baron, 2005), research on its basic premise that overconformity undermines good judgment (Kerr and Tindale, 2004; Paulus, 1998; Turner and Pratkanis, 1998; Whyte, 1998) suggests that understanding how norm processes operate within small units can have important consequences, especially when considering culpability for legal violations. Expanding research on battlefield crime to emphasize unit behavior ". . . may reveal a better means of structuring military justice and achieving accountability on the battlefield without what seems to be a lopsided emphasis on the individual, and (in several recent military justice cases), on the junior military members involved in the incident" (Puckett and Attwood, 2012, p. 84).

5. *In novel situations, the values (and attitudes) of a social group guide but do not necessarily predict normative behavior.*

Army operations are dynamic, and as a result it is not uncommon for soldiers to encounter novel situations in which previous experience may not be particularly useful in guiding action. In these instances, there is no normative behavior and the military relies on formal "leadership" in unit decision-making processes; a leader makes decisions that set the standard for normative behavior (see Chapter 4). However, in reality, norm development is much more egalitarian and decentralized (e.g., everyone is a leader; everyone is a follower) (Tuckman, 1965; Fine, 2001). It is important to consider the development of a norm as a group process. An important body of research in this regard highlights how social groups "negotiate" norms by continuously defining the "meaning" of member behaviors relative to the group's values and ideals (Fine, 2001).

Although values are different from norms, understanding the relationship between the two in norm formation is important. All Army personnel are expected to uphold the Seven Core Army Values; therefore, in novel situations these values are supposed to guide norm assessments negotiated among group members. The group determines how behaviors associated with a task are to be accomplished in ways that conform to its core values. But values are not behaviors, and norms require effective communication to group members. As a component of how norms form (i.e., how they are communicated among group members) it is equally relevant to consider dissemination and diffusion. Without understanding the relationship between values and norm development, as well as the dissemination of norms, it becomes difficult to predict the norms that might emerge from novel situations.

THEMES FOR RESEARCH ON NORMS

A number of features about the Army have implications for researching social norms. First, the Army is also an "all volunteer" force with a self-selection process of members joining a professional organization with a strong sense of established organizational values. Second, the military is a "total institution" (Goffman, 1961), meaning all elements of a soldier's life are under military control. To direct the social norms of its members, the Army has its own laws, rules, policy, doctrine, ethics, and values, as well as codes of conduct. Everyone in the Army is formally indoctrinated in this lifestyle. Furthermore, these expectations apply whether a soldier is on or off duty, and they distinguish a military versus civilian career. A soldier is always expected to behave in a manner that upholds military honor (e.g., behaviors such as adultery are punishable through military courts).

Second, Army units are idiosyncratic social groups. Members often live together; operate in an extensive variety of contexts; collaborate with different groups (see Chapter 6); deploy for extended periods of time; work under the duress of potential trauma, injury, or death; and may use lethal force. Complicating matters, soldiers rely on one another for their survival, yet units frequently and regularly rotate membership and leadership personnel (see Chapter 4). Soldiers are also required to accomplish missions that may have contradictory objectives (e.g., one day performing a peacekeeping mission to protect civilians, the next day killing enemy combatants).

Finally, due to the hierarchical structure of the military, social groups are nested. This implies that social norms may also be nested (i.e., squad within a company within a battalion) such that small units from different higher-level units potentially may express slightly different norms.

Although studies of social norms within the Army have been limited, case study research in this area has investigated the context of small units in combat (Stouffer, 1949; Marshall, 1947; Gabriel and Savage, 1979) as well as social norms associated with life on military installations (Hawkins, 2005; MacLeish, 2013). Here the committee emphasizes again, as noted in the report's first recommendation, that the most effective way to research norms within Army units is to conduct research activities with active duty Army personnel.

FUTURE RESEARCH ON NORMS

With a scientifically informed understanding of social norms, the roles they play in individual and group behavior, and the processes through which they form and change, the Army will be much better equipped to resolve norm-based conflicts and ensure that the Seven Core Army Values are sustained in units' social norms. The center of a soldier's universe is the squad and platoon. Group bonding occurs or fails at this level, group norms are defined and evolve, and standards of behavior are set. It is at this level that relationships are formed and that much of the Army's mission effectiveness is determined.

Conclusion 2

The committee concludes that norms are an important dimension of the social context within small units. Due to the unique conditions of military contexts, the committee further concludes that participants in research studies on military norms must be active duty soldiers, if the results are to be meaningful in real military environments.

Recommendation 2
The U.S. Army Research Institute for the Behavioral and Social Sciences (ARI) and other relevant U.S. military funding agencies should fund basic research that:

1. **identifies the content of norms; the values, attitudes, and behaviors that express norms; formal and informal incentives and sanctions that maintain norms; conditions that moderate norm-relevant behavior; and the development of norms over time;**
2. **examines the relationship between norms and the performance of soldiers and the attitudes and behaviors of their leaders; and**
3. **identifies approaches for changing norms to produce more effective soldiers and units.**

To facilitate the research program on norms, the committee recommends that ARI establish a multidisciplinary task force charged with development of a program of research studying norms in military contexts.

REFERENCES

Ajzen, I., and M. Fishbein. (1980). *Understanding Attitudes and Predicting Social Behavior.* Englewood Cliffs, NJ: Prentice-Hall.

Axelrod, R.M. (1986). An evolutionary approach to norms. *American Political Science Review,* 80(4):1,095-1,111.

Baron, R.S. (2005). So right, it's wrong: Groupthink and the ubiquitous nature of polarized decision making. *Advances in Experimental Social Psychology,* 37:219-253.

Bendor, J., and P. Swistak. (2001). The evolution of norms. *American Journal of Sociology,* 106(6):1,493-1,545.

Bicchieri, C. (2006). *The Grammar of Society: The Nature and Dynamics of Social Norms.* Cambridge, UK: Cambridge University Press.

Brainerd, C.J., and V.F. Reyna. (1990). Gist is the grist: Fuzzy-trace theory and the new intuitionism. *Developmental Review,* 10(1):3-47.

Chaiken, S., and Y. Trope. (1999). *Dual-process Theories in Social Psychology.* New York: Guilford Press.

Cialdini, R.B. (1988). *Influence: Science and Practice,* 2nd ed. Glenview, IL: Scott, Foresman.

Cialdini, R.B., and M.R. Trost. (1998). Social influence: Social norms, conformity and compliance. In D.T. Gilbert, S.T. Fiske, and G. Lindzey, Eds., *The Handbook of Social Psychology,* 4th ed., Vol. 2 (pp. 151-192). New York: McGraw-Hill.

Cialdini, R.B., R.R. Reno, and C.A. Kallgren. (1990). A focus theory of normative conduct: Recycling the concept of norms to reduce littering in public space. *Journal of Personality and Social Psychology,* 58(10):1,015-1,026.

Coleman, J.S. (1990). *Foundations of Social Theory.* Cambridge, MA: Belknap Press.

Epstein, S. (1990). Cognitive-experiential self-theory. In L. Pervin, Ed., *Handbook of Personality: Theory and Research* (pp. 165-192). New York: Guilford Publications.
Evans, J.St.B.T. (2007). On the resolution of conflict in dual process theories of reasoning. *Thinking and Reasoning,* 13(4):321-339.
Evans, J.St.B.T. (2008). Dual-processing accounts of reasoning, judgment, and social cognition. *Annual Review of Psychology,* 59:255-278.
Evans, J.St.B.T. (2010). Intuition and reasoning: A dual-process perspective. *Psychological Inquiry,* 21(4):313-326.
Evans, J.St.B.T. (2012). Questions and challenges for the new psychology of reasoning. *Thinking and Reasoning,* 18(1):5-31.
Fine, G.A. (2001). Enacting norms: Mushrooming and the culture of expectations and explanations. In M. Hechter and K.D. Opp, Eds., *Social Norms* (pp. 139-164). New York: Russell Sage Foundation.
Fishbein, M., and I. Ajzen. (1975). *Belief, Attitude, Intention, and Behavior: An Introduction to Theory and Research.* Reading, MA: Addison-Wesley.
Fishbein, M., and I. Ajzen. (1977). Attitude-behavior relations: A theoretical analysis and review of empirical research. *Psychological Bulletin,* 84:888-918.
Gabriel, R.A., and P.L. Savage. (1979). *Crisis in Command: Mismanagement in the Army.* New York: Hill and Wang.
Gailliot, M.T., S.A. Gitter, M.D. Baker, and R.F. Baumeister. (2012). Breaking the rules: Low trait or state self-control increases social norm violations. *Psychology,* 3(12):1,074-1,083.
Goffman, E. (1961). *Asylums: Essays on the Social Situation of Mental Patients and Other Inmates.* Garden City, NY: Anchor Books.
Greene, J.D., S.A. Morelli, K. Lowenberg, L.E. Nystrom, and J.D. Cohen. (2008). Cognitive load selectively interferes with utilitarian moral judgment. *Cognition,* 107(3):1,144-1,154.
Hawkins, J.P. (2005). *Army of Hope, Army of Alienation: Culture and Contradiction in the American Army Community of Cold War Germany*, 2nd ed. Tuscaloosa: University of Alabama Press.
Hechter, M., and K.D. Opp. (2001). *Social Norms.* New York: Russell Sage Foundation.
Heckathorn, D.D. (1990). Collective sanctions and compliance norms: A formal theory of group-mediated social control. *American Sociological Review,* 55:366-384.
Hoffman, L. (1995). *The Vertical is not yet Becoming the Horizontal.* Report No. A201144. Washington, DC: National War College.
Homans, G.C. (1950). *The Human Group.* New York: Harcourt, Brace.
Horne, C. (2009). *The Rewards of Punishment: A Relational Theory of Norm Enforcement.* Stanford, CA: Stanford University Press.
Janis, I.L. (1972). *Victims of Groupthink: A Psychological Study of Foreign-Policy Decisions and Fiascos.* Boston, MA: Houghton, Mifflin.
Kahneman, D. (2012). *Thinking Fast and Slow.* London, UK: Penguin Books.
Kahneman, D., and S. Frederick. (2005). A model of heuristic judgment. In K.J. Holyoak and R.G. Morrison, Eds., *The Cambridge Handbook of Thinking and Reasoning* (pp. 267-293). New York: Cambridge University Press.
Kahneman, D., and A. Tversky. (1984). Choices, values, and frames. *American Psychologist,* 39(4):341-350.
Keizer, K., S. Lindenberg, and L. Steg. (2008). The spreading of disorder. *Science,* 322(5908): 1,681-1,685.
Kerr, N.L., and R.S. Tindale. (2004). Group performance and decision making. *Annual Review of Psychology,* 55:623-655.
MacLeish, K.T. (2013). *Making War at Fort Hood: Life and Uncertainty in a Military Community.* Princeton, NJ: Princeton University Press.

Marshall, S.L.A. (1947). *Men Against Fire: The Problem of Battle Command in Future War.* New York: Morrow.

Martens, M.H., and M.R.J. Fox. (2007). Do familiarity and expectations change perception? Drivers' glances and responses to changes. *Transportation Research Part F: Psychology and Behaviour,* 10(6):476-492.

Moorhead, G. (1982). Groupthink: Hypothesis in need of testing. *Group and Organization Management,* 7(4):429-444.

Murdoch, M., J.B. Pryor, M.A. Polusny, G.D. Grackstetter, and D.C. Ripley. (2009). Local social norms and military sexual stressors: Do senior officers' norms matter? *Military Medicine,* 174(10):1,100-1,104.

Opp, K.D. (2001). Social networks and the emergence of protest norms. In M. Hechter and K.D. Opp, Eds., *Social Norms* (pp. 139-164). New York: Russell Sage Foundation.

Parsons, T. (1951). *The Social System.* London, UK: Routledge and Kegan Paul.

Paulus, P.B. (1998). Developing consensus about Groupthink after all these years. *Organizational Behavior and Human Decision Processes,* 73(2/3):362-374.

Puckett, N.A., and M. Atwood. (2012). Crime on the battlefield: Military fate or individual choice? In J.H. Laurence and M.D. Matthews, Eds., *The Oxford Handbook of Military Psychology* (pp. 79-91). New York: Oxford University Press.

Reyna, V. (2004). How people make decisions that involve risk a dual-process approach. *Current Directions in Psychological Science,* 13(2):60-66.

Schulze, W., A. Maertens, and B. Wansink. (2013). Eating dogfood: Examining the relative roles of reason and emotion. *Journal of Economic Behavior and Organization,* 92:202-213.

Shiv, B., and A. Fedorikhin. (1999). Heart and mind in conflict: The interplay of affect and cognition in consumer decision making. *Journal of Consumer Research,* 26(3):278-292.

Sills, D.L., and R.K. Merton, Eds. (1968). *International Encyclopedia of the Social Sciences.* New York: Macmillan.

Sloman, S.A. (1996). The empirical case for two systems of reasoning. *Psychological Bulletin,* 119:3-22.

Stanovich, K.E. (1999). *Who Is Rational? Studies of Individual Differences in Reasoning.* Mahway, NJ: Lawrence Erlbaum Associates.

Stouffer, S.A. (1949). *The American Solider: Adjustment During Army Life.* Princeton, NJ: Princeton University Press.

Tajfel, H. (1981). *Human Groups and Social Categories.* Cambridge, UK: Cambridge University Press.

Tuckman, B.W. (1965). Developmental sequence in small groups. *Psychological Bulletin,* 63(6):384-399.

Turner, J.C., M.A. Hogg, P.J. Oakes, S.D. Reicher, and M.S. Wetherell. (1987). *Rediscovering the Social Group: A Self-Categorization Theory.* New York: Basil Blackwell.

Turner, M.E., and A.R. Pratkanis. (1998). Twenty-five years of Groupthink theory and research: Lessons from the evaluation of a theory. *Organizational Behavior and Human Decision Processes,* 73(2/3):105-115.

Ullman-Margalit, E. (1977). *The Emergence of Norms.* Oxford, UK: Clarendon Press.

Whyte, G. (1998). Recasting Janis's Groupthink model: The key role of collective efficacy in decision fiascoes. *Organizational Behavior and Human Decision Processes,* 73(2/3):185-209.

Willer, R., K. Kuwabara, and M.W. Macy. (2009). The false enforcement of unpopular norms. *American Journal of Sociology,* 115:451-490.

Wimbush, J.C., and J.M. Shepard. (1994). Toward an understanding of ethical climate: Its relationship to ethical behavior and supervisory influence. *Journal of Business Ethics,* 13(8):637-647.

Wong, K. (2014, January 10). Military cracks down on "locker room talk." *The Hill*, Available: http://thehill.com/blogs/defcon-hill/policy-strategy/195083-military-cracks-down-on-locker-room-talk-at-academies#ixzz2qE1ZPsra [April 2014].

Young, P.H. (1996). The economics of convention. *Journal of Economic Perspectives*, 10(2): 105-122.

3

Environmental Transitions

People are creatures of habit. Life transitions—whether to a different city, a different organization, or even a different job within an organization—can be disorienting and undermine performance and health. U.S. military personnel in the 21st century face transitions on a scale unprecedented in other aspects of life, even when compared with soldiers just a decade ago. Attending to the impact of transitions will allow the Army to assess a variety of questions, such as:

- What personal (e.g., personality traits, beliefs, and habits) and organizational (e.g., organizational structures and routines) characteristics increase service members' resilience and operational effectiveness in the face of transitions?
- Are there ways to instill service members with certain habits during training so that they can more seamlessly transition between one environment and the next?
- What is known about the formation of habits that are functional in one environment but dysfunctional in another? How can habits be deactivated upon transition to an environment in which they are no longer functional? Can one deactivate individual habits that were learned and functional in one environmental context but are dysfunctional in another?
- Can advanced simulation technology be informed by, and help inform, a science-based understanding of how transitions and contextual cues interact with learning and performance?

- How do personal and organizational characteristics interact with each other to determine a unit's operational effectiveness?

While soldiers who opt for full 20-year (or more) military careers may enjoy a sense of stability from a career trajectory within a single large organization with well-defined career paths and promotion processes, many other factors conspire to make military careers extremely unsettled. Military downsizing, attrition, increased mission tempo, relocations through deployments and permanent changes of station, continually morphing units, and new communication and transportation technology both enable and incentivize military leaders to demand unmatched flexibility, adaptability, and mobility from today's soldiers. Unfortunately, increasing the pace of life transitions can come at a high psychological and physical cost (see, e.g., Pincus et al., 2001). Understanding how to mitigate these negative consequences while retaining their benefits is a basic research challenge for the military.

A soldier's life is punctuated with transitions. With the nation currently engaged in multiple conflicts and other military operations across the globe, a soldier's career is organized into a series of permanent duty station moves and temporary deployments wherein soldiers are moved from home station to a position of readiness to engage or support military operations. Even a single deployment can involve multiple transitions. For example, Pincus and colleagues (2001) define five stages of deployment (predeployment, deployment, sustainment, redeployment, and postdeployment), with each stage characterized by different cognitive, social, and emotional challenges for soldiers and their families.

While the psychological and physical costs of repeated deployments to Iraq and Afghanistan over the past decade have received much public attention, other significant environmental transitions are experienced by soldiers around the world. For example, a paper on Army teams prepared for the committee by Captain Andrew Miller (former U.S. Army)[1] describes the author's experience during a 365-day assignment to the Republic of Korea beginning in 2006: "The arrival and departure processing takes 1-2 weeks on each end of the tour due to mandatory briefings, classes, paperwork, appointments, doctor visits, packing/load personal property, etc. Factor in as well the mid-tour leave (up to 30 days normally) that soldiers take, and a billet 'filled' for 12 months might only be functional for 9 to 10 of those months" (p. 16). Furthermore, in Miller's experience and consistent with other military service members who spoke with the committee, even expected transitions can suddenly take an unexpected direction. For example, Miller describes a circumstance in which soldiers stationed in Korea

[1]Paper available by request from this study's public access file.

(who have the expectation of being exempt from deployment to Iraq and Afghanistan during this tour) were deployed to Iraq: "All soldiers assigned to the brigade deployed, to include soldiers departing Korea in less than 2 weeks" (p. 17). Miller notes that soldiers assigned to this brigade in Korea were rarely accompanied by spouses or family, and dependents were not authorized by the Army. Consequently, "soldiers endured 'back to back' deployments away from their families, not counting their 10 days of leave shoehorned into deployment wrap-up" (p. 17). The committee can imagine severe psychological implications on soldiers separated from their loved ones and expecting to transition home within a few weeks or months, only to find themselves deployed to a war zone for the next year.[2]

Each of these transitions can undermine unit effectiveness and undermine the performance and health of individual soldiers. For example, data show that "[s]oldiers are particularly vulnerable to becoming a fatality within the first three months of deployment" with almost 40 percent of fatalities occurring during this time (Plank et al., 2010, p. 2,299). Subsequent data have shown that one-half of the injuries sustained by a Marine infantry battalion occurred within the first 50 days of its deployment to Afghanistan (Phillips et al., 2013). Furthermore, the effects of deployment do not end when soldiers return home. After transitioning back from deployment, soldiers often exhibit anger, alienation, and unhealthy behaviors. For example, postdeployment soldiers show more risk-taking (e.g., unsafe driving or unprotected sex) and more unhealthy habits (e.g., eating junk food or drinking alcohol), even when controlling for the well-documented increase in posttraumatic stress (PTS) following deployment (Adler et al., 2011b). It has also been shown that multiple deployments can compound these effects. For example, previously deployed soldiers were found to be three times as likely to screen positive for PTS and major depression and 90 percent more likely to score below the general population norm on physical functioning as soldiers with no previous deployments (Kline et al., 2010).

Given that the factors driving the pace of transitions within the military are unlikely to disappear (and indeed, they seem to be increasing in

[2]The committee recognizes that drastic changes to expected transitions such as that described by Miller are not experienced by all soldiers, and in fact, the Army has gone to great length to establish clear expectations for regular and repeated transitions. Specifically, the Army Force Generation regulation usually provides a level of predictability to the process of unit formation, training, and assignments. It regulates a 3-year cycle of designating cohorts of soldiers and leaders within units, in order to establish cycles of (1) arriving to a unit at generally the same time in order to develop as a cohesive team through training in the first year, (2) availability for worldwide deployment in the second year, and (3) time available for necessary recovery and subsequent relocation to a new duty station in the third year (see Department of the Army, 2011).

prevalence in the general population as well), it is crucial that research uncover the mechanisms underlying the negative consequences associated with transitions and suggest interventions to preempt or repair them. From this perspective, it is useful to distinguish local/specific consequences of transitions from more global/generic consequences. In the former type of consequence, when an individual or team transitions from one specific environment to another, the transition can have consequences that are associated particularly with the environments transferred to, from, or both. For example, when a soldier transitions from home station to deployment, old adaptive behaviors (e.g., regular healthy meals and portion sizes) may fall away and new adaptive behaviors (e.g., vigilance) may not be sufficiently activated. In the latter type of transition consequence, simply the act of making a transition (any transition) can undermine operational effectiveness and health, for example, by increasing stress. Local and global consequences clearly interact. For example, the disruption of healthy habits may partly explain why transitions increase stress. In this chapter, the committee reviews research that addresses both local and global consequences of military transitions, and we offer specific recommendations for a basic research agenda to advance the state of knowledge in these areas.

STATE OF RESEARCH ON TRANSITION CONSEQUENCES

Although people are creatures of habit, they frequently confront change. Several lines of research have examined how individuals and organizations respond to such changes. Although primarily developed in civilian contexts, this research has relevance to many of the issues confronted by soldiers and military organizations; indeed, it is already informing current military practices for reducing the challenges of transition, at least with respect to individuals' mental health (see, for example, Cornum et al., 2011). This research provides a solid foundation for a "science of transitions," but it speaks only indirectly to the full range of challenges confronted by military transitions and the consequences these have for both the individual and the organization. Here we outline the current state of this research as well as promising directions to enhance its relevance for military challenges.

Local and Specific Effects of Transitions (The Role of Habit and Routine)

When an individual or small unit transitions from one environment to another, the transition can create immediate and specific consequences. Well-honed skills and routines may fail to transfer to the new situation. On the other hand, behaviors that serve the individual well in one context (e.g., hypervigilance on the battlefield) might persist into a new context where they are no longer adaptive (e.g., hypervigilance at home with family, postdeployment). A large body of research, highlighted below, has documented the context specificity of human decision making and the challenges this presents when individuals and organizations must transition to new circumstances. Research has also examined the mechanisms underlying these effects, emphasizing that, when situations are stable, decisions and behaviors become automatized, which allows for efficient decision making, frees up cognitive effort for other areas, and is arguably a necessary property of effective decision making in general (Bargh and Chartrand, 1999; Gigerenzer and Goldstein, 1996), even if it creates difficulties when transitioning across stable situations. In contrast, there is a paucity of research on how to mitigate these consequences of environmental shifts when change becomes the norm.

The notion that individuals (Wood et al., 2005), organizations (Becker, 2004), and even whole economies (Nelson and Winter, 1982) organize their activities around regular patterns of behavior, each of which "is followed repeatedly, but is subject to change if conditions change" (Winter, 1964, p. 263) has a rich tradition across the behavioral sciences (see Chapter 2 discussion of norms as regular patterns of behavior). When the individual is the unit of analysis, these patterns are typically referred to as *habits*. When the organization is the unit of analysis, these patterns are called *routines*. In either case, the patterns are defined by several generally accepted characteristics: (1) they repeat; (2) they are "automatic" in the sense that people follow them with little conscious attention and they do not require substantial cognitive resources (Kahneman, 2003; Simon, 1982);[3] (3) they are context dependent, meaning they are only evoked within specific situations, locations, or relationships (see, e.g., Kahneman and Miller, 1986); and (4) these default habits and routines are resistant to change (March and Simon, 1958).

For example, at the individual level, habits can be seen as a behavioral manifestation of the status quo bias—a preference for the current set of behaviors rather than making a change. Preference for the status quo has been explained as the reference point against which change is measured, and since losses are more psychologically salient than gains (Kahneman and Tversky, 1979), the potential loss from change becomes more salient than the potential gain from change, creating a preference for whatever is currently in play (Samuelson and Zeckhauser, 1988). A related notion is regret avoidance: since people experience greater regret for action than for inaction (Kahneman et al., 1982), they will tend to choose the status

[3]However, in the context of organizational research, some have argued that routines are "effortful accomplishments" (Feldman and Pentland, 2003) that require thought and improvisation in that, at least at the organizational level, contexts are too varied to allow automaticity in the traditional sense.

quo—doing what they have always done. There is also evidence for an existence bias (Eidelman and Crandall, 2012): simply having an existing habit suggests that the habit is a good one. This bias is reminiscent of the adage credited to Bert Lance, "if it ain't broke, don't fix it."

Similarly, at the organizational level, practices, routines, and strategies tend to become institutionalized such that organizations reduce search activities aimed at identifying innovative practices (Lant, 1992; March and Simon, 1958). These institutionalized routines are sticky, in the sense that only in the face of large organizational failures do people question their existence (Cyert and March, 1963). Failure motivates organizations to increase their search activities and to accept new practices that differ from their existing routines—"non-local" search (Levinthal and March, 1981)—thus allowing for new routines and practices (March, 1981). These characteristics of habits and routines (automatic, contextually generated but sticky) explain their central relevance to transitions research. (See also the discussion in Chapter 4 of the role new soldiers play in changing small-group dynamics.)

Transitioning from one environment to another threatens the viability of old habits and routines. First, old habits and routines can persist in new situations where they are meaningless and/or unproductive, in that they can be conditioned on irrelevant contextual features that persist in this new situation (Grant, 1996). Second, beneficial habits and routines can extinguish as people become removed from their original context—for instance, habits associated with particular times, environments, moods, or group members (Bower and Forgas, 2000; Wood et al., 2005). From this perspective, transitions serve to disrupt the stimulus cues that trigger routinized behavior (Wood et al., 2005). Transitions can eliminate certain cues for adaptive behaviors, such as training or exercise, such that these behaviors are no longer automatically cued and must fall back on effortful intentional control before they can become routinized in the new context. Conversely, cues for automatic behavior may be present in the new context, yet the behavior itself may no longer be adaptive (such as hypervigilance responses to loud noises when back at home station).

Although most research has focused on the negative consequences of transitions, they create positive opportunities as well. For example, individuals more easily adopt beneficial habits following environmental transition, at least when strong internal or organizational values help motivate the desire for behavior change (Verplanken et al., 2008; see also Chapter 2).

Although the mechanisms underlying habits and routines are reasonably well understood, research is still needed on how to mitigate the negative consequences and exploit the opportunities of habitual reasoning in the face of repetitive change. Several gaps in the literature limit the military's (and organizations more generally) ability to translate findings on habits into beneficial practices to manage their effects.

At a basic level, research is needed simply to document and classify the most common habits and routines that are impacted by environmental transitions and the nature of this impact. For example, which classes of beneficial habits are typically disrupted or enhanced when moving to a new environment? Which classes inappropriately persist into the new environment? Which maladaptive habits should be targeted for extinction in the context of a transition?

Then, for each of these classes of behavior, what theoretical findings can inform decisions on how to select, train, or organize personnel to maximize the benefit and minimize the harm that arises from these phenomena? For example, the fact that transitions can disrupt "good" behavior suggests the need for more extensive research on the types of cues upon which such behaviors are conditioned and on whether techniques or organizational practices exist that help preserve these cues across contexts. To the extent that different contexts require different habits, research is required to understand how to contextualize these behaviors more appropriately. For example, should they be contextualized through improved alignment of the contextual elicitors of habits and routines with the contexts where they are needed, through training simulations that allow people to practice transitions, or through metacognitive skills that make individuals more aware of the determinants of their behavior?

Finally, in that military routines and habits are often established in facsimiles of the operational environment (e.g., roleplaying exercise and, increasingly, computer simulations), more research is needed to ensure these simulations are informed by a science-based understanding of how transitions and contextual cues interact with learning and performance. An oft-stated goal underlying the development of such simulations is that they should replicate all aspects of the physical, social, and emotional context with perfect fidelity to facilitate learning transfer. While laudable, this goal is unattainable for the foreseeable future, given the current state of the art in modeling human behavior (e.g., see National Research Council, 2008a, 2008b). Rather, the committee believes that simulation methods and technologies need to be informed by a better understanding of the key sensory and situational cues that trigger and reinforce desirable soldier behavior within military contexts. For instance, rather than focusing on improving all aspects of simulation fidelity, fidelity should be prioritized by an understanding of which cues are minimally necessary to ensure that appropriate habits and routines are elicited in the actual operational environment. In addressing these research questions, simulation technology may actually serve as an important methodological tool to advance science-based understanding of how transitions and contextual cues interact with learning. For example, in that simulation technology allows a researcher to systematically manipulate levels of fidelity (the degree to which the simulation duplicates a real military environment) and the presence or absence of contextual cues, it can serve as a powerful tool for empirical research on habits and routines.

In summary, further research on the local and specific effects of transitions could help to address the following questions:

- Which desirable individual habits or organizational routines, especially those prevalent within military contexts, interact poorly with transitions?
- What theories explain how individuals and groups deactivate habits that were learned and functional in one context but are dysfunctional in another context?
- Are there ways to instill service members with certain desirable habits during training so that they can more seamlessly transition between one context and the next; if not, are there efficient ways to recontextualize or reactivate the desirable habits in a new context?
- What individual habits transcend context in providing a positive benefit in multiple environments? How can organizational routines be used to prime and reinforce these habits? For example, can such habits be preserved by reinforcing strong organizational values that are made salient across contexts and that reinforce the desired habits?
- How can interdisciplinary partnerships between advanced training technology (e.g., virtual reality) and theories on routines and habits be established to further research and improve training? For instance, can virtual technology be used as a methodological tool to study the contextualization of habits, with the results from such studies used to inform the design of training systems with an improved theoretical understanding of the contextual nature of habits and routines?

Global and Generic Effects of Transitions (the Role of Resilience)

Whereas research on routines and habits emphasizes the local and specific negative consequences of environmental transitions, other research has emphasized that the mere occurrence of transitions, especially repeated transitions, can produce broad and generalized deficits to individual and organizational performance (see, for example, Kline et al., 2010). And whereas research on local consequences emphasizes the importance of repeated patterns of behavior, research on the global consequences of change emphasizes the role of stress (Cornum et al., 2011). From this perspective, change acts as a stressor that ultimately breaks down the integrity of individuals and organizations. Essentially, transitions serve as psychological "shocks" that can drain physical and mental health and lead to psychological distress (e.g., PTS), maladaptive behaviors (e.g., sexual assault), long-term health effects, and organizational dysfunction (Kline et al., 2010).

Although the bulk of past research, especially as it relates to individuals, has focused on treatment (for example, developing improved screening instruments for pathology and improved therapeutic regimens) that repairs the consequences of these shocks, a more recent line of research has begun to emphasize a proactive, prevention-based approach known as promoting *psychological resilience* (Peterson, 2006; Luthar et al., 2000). Rather than focusing strictly on pathology, this alternative emphasizes individual and organizational strengths that inoculate individuals against the negative effects of stress.

The concept of psychological resilience, which occurs across a range of fields in the behavioral sciences, arose as a way of explaining why similar environmental stressors had very different consequences for different individuals. In trauma research, the construct of resilience is used to explain why some individuals are able to thrive in the face of traumatic stress or adverse conditions that overwhelm most others (Peterson, 2006). Within developmental psychology, resilience was evoked to explain why some children developed normally even in the presence of environmental stressors such as extreme poverty (e.g., Fraser, 1997). In research on organizations, a construct similar to resilience, *psychological capital,* is used to describe why groups and institutions thrive in the face of adversity (Luthans et al., 2007). What is common across these perspectives is a focus on identifying cognitive, social, and emotional characteristics of individuals that enable them to thrive and flourish in the face of stress (Fredrickson, 2003). There is also convergence with regard to the factors that predict resilience, including the role of positive emotions, the role of individual abilities such as coping skills, and the importance of positive institutions and social relationships (e.g., Cacioppo et al., 2011).

Resilience is already a focus of Department of Defense research and practice (for recent reviews see Adler et al., 2011a; Meredith et al., 2011). For example, the U.S. Army's Comprehensive Soldier and Family Fitness program is informed by resilience research and claims the stress of transitions can be mitigated by inculcating emotional, social, family, and spiritual fitness (Algoe and Fredrickson, 2011; Cornum et al., 2011). This program attempts to buffer the global impact of transitions by teaching soldiers various skills and techniques to improve resilience (Cornum et al., 2011). Key elements of the program include periodic assessments of soldier resilience through a self-reported instrument known as the Global Assessment Tool (Peterson et al., 2011), universal resilience training, training "master resilience trainers," follow-up and periodic reassessment, and tracking of resilience throughout the career of Army personnel. Several Army-funded studies have attempted to assess soldier fitness and examine how this changes across broad transitions such as predeployment to deployment and subsequently to postdeployment (Park, 2012).

The Comprehensive Soldier and Family Fitness program is just one of many attempts to incorporate resilience concepts within military organizations. For example, a recent RAND report reviewed 23 Department of Defense programs that promote psychological resilience among service members (Meredith et al., 2011). This report emphasized that, although there is scientific evidence that resilience-related factors improve resilience to stress (especially individual-level factors such as positive thinking, positive affect, positive coping, realism, and behavioral control), there is far less evidence that resilience-enhancing programs are effective in military contexts. Thus, effective ways to translate these research findings remain an active research challenge.

Despite these early promising findings, there are fundamental limitations in resilience research that must be overcome to increase the relevance of the concept to military contexts. Much current research on resilience treats psychological resilience as a trait individuals possesses, albeit one that can be improved with training. This is especially true of the body of research underlying current Department of Defense resilience programs (Cornum et al., 2011). In contrast, other research has adopted the perspective that resilience is not an individual trait but is best seen as a quality that arises from the interaction of the individual with the environment. For example, Seccombe (2002, p. 385) writes, "The widely held view of resiliency as an individual disposition, family trait, or community phenomenon is insufficient . . . resiliency cannot be understood or improved in significant ways by merely focusing on these individual-level factors." Similarly, Gilligan (2001, p. 94) argues, "The degree of resilience displayed by a person in a certain context may be said to be related to the extent to which that context has elements that nurture this resilience." As an example of this divergence of perspectives, the Comprehensive Soldier and Family Fitness Program emphasizes the importance of individual traits such as "grit"—the willingness to persist in the face of failure—as traits to inculcate on the basis of research showing it predicts successful completion of basic training (Duckworth et al., 2007). Yet persistence in the face of failure may cause problems when prior skills and practice are inappropriate to a new organization or culture and when adaptability may be more valued. Emphasizing the interaction of resilience traits with environments moves the study of resilience away from a study of individual differences and toward thinking about resilience as context dependent. The committee believes understanding the contextual limits of resilience (and how to overcome them) is a promising direction for future research.

By restricting the focus to individual differences, resilience research has also underexplored the utility of the construct for groups and organizations. Most resilience research treats the individual as the unit of analysis and downplays the group or organizational levels of analysis. For example, of the 270 publications reviewed by the RAND report on resilience, only 13 examined organizational-level factors related to resilience (Meredith et al., 2011). There are at least two ways that group-level constructs can enrich the concept of resilience. The first, and most common, is to consider how group-level factors can improve the functioning of the individual. For example, *social resilience* can be defined as "the *individual's* capacity to work with others" (Cacioppo et al., 2011). The other, and perhaps more relevant approach for military contexts, is to treat the organization as an entity that can be resilient in ways analogous to the individual. For example, some research uses the term *psychological capital* to describe the resilience of an organization, although it typically defines the resilience of the group as simply the sum of the resilience of its individual members (Luthans et al., 2007). More radical proposals suggest that the group should be seen as a unit of analysis that cannot be predicted solely in terms of properties of individuals. For example, organizational effectiveness may be best predicted by considering group-level factors as perceptions of individuals influenced by interpersonal factors such as social contagion (Clapp-Smith et al., 2009; see also Walumbwa et al., 2011). Other research has considered a society or community as a unit of analysis, although this work often appeals to ecological, rather than psychological, mechanisms to predict resilience to stress (Adger, 2000). In that soldiers are organized into and strongly identify with small units, and given the rich tapestry of formal and informal hierarchies found within military organizations, the committee believes expanding the construct of resilience to encompass such groups is a promising direction for future research.

The committee believes research on resilience is a promising direction for alleviating the stresses of environmental transitions; however, the current focus of recent research on individual antecedents and traits, why certain individuals are resilient to obstacles, and the consequences of resilience limits these potential benefits. Further research in this area could help to address the following questions:

- What are the contextual limits of resilience and how can they be overcome? For example, how does resilience vary across environments and arise from the interaction of individual traits and situational factors?

- What are the group or organizational antecedents of resilience such as group bonds, leadership style, and organizational values?
- What theories might explain how individual resilience relates to consequences at the organizational level? For example, is the effectiveness of an organization strictly increased by enhancing the resilience of its constituent members, or might factors that improve individual health undermine organizational effectiveness?
- How do individual-level findings on resilience translate to the organizational level of analysis? For example, are there organizational analogues of the traits that explain why individuals are successful in the face of adversity?

Local and Global Consequences Clearly Interact

Finally, although the committee has discussed the local and global consequences of transitions as separate research questions (and they have largely been treated separately within behavioral science research), examining these questions *together* may yield further insights into how transitions impact soldier performance. For example, although environmental transitions tend to increase stress, the nature of this stress (and the specific resilience-building techniques required to buffer against it) may depend on which specific habits or routines are affected. Resilience and habit research bring two different levels of analysis to the same phenomena, and considering how these levels interact can lead to a better understanding of both global and local consequences of change. Research that combines these two perspectives could help to address the following questions:

- Does the disruption of healthy habits following transitions help explain why transitions increase stress? For example, does an environmental transition lead to a general (albeit temporary) shift from automatic to more deliberative thinking, with a consequent increase in cognitive load and cognitive depletion, and thus explain increases in general stress? Alternatively, or perhaps in combination, does the disruption of beneficial habits (such as exercise, predictable sleep patterns, and healthy meals) undermine cognitive and physical functioning?
- To the extent that good habits tend to be disrupted following an environmental transition, is there value in taking a resilience approach to analysis of this phenomenon? For example, rather than focusing on this as a pathology that should be treated, what positive traits or skills might explain why this does not occur in some individuals or organizational units? Are there social or organizational factors that encourage good behavior through transitions?

- Given that traits adaptive in one context sometimes persist into inappropriate contexts, are there positive traits or skills that explain why this does not occur in some individuals or between some contexts?
- How do organizational routines support or detract from the resilience of organizations in the face of adversity?

FUTURE RESEARCH ON ENVIRONMENTAL TRANSITIONS

Conclusion 3

The committee concludes that the repeated environmental transitions faced by military personnel create significant challenges and opportunities to operational effectiveness and resilience.

Recommendation 3

The U.S. Army Research Institute for the Behavioral and Social Sciences and other U.S. military funding agencies should support basic research on:

1. **individual habits and organizational routines that are disrupted by environmental transitions, including research into the positive and negative consequences of these disruptions within specific military contexts and that examines how these consequences might be proactively managed to increase unit and soldier effectiveness;**
2. **the interaction between individual characteristics and features of groups and organizations, with the aim of predicting resilience; how this interaction may differ across types of environments; and groups and organizations, as well as individuals, as the unit of analysis; and**
3. **exploring in what ways and under what conditions local disruption of habits affects global consequences for resilience.**

REFERENCES

Adger, W.N. (2000). Social and ecological resilience: Are they related? *Progress in Human Geography,* 24(3):347-364.

Adler, A.B., P.D. Bliese, and C.A. Castro. (2011a). *Deployment Psychology: Evidence-Based Strategies to Promote Mental Health in the Military.* Washington, DC: American Psychological Association.

Adler, A.B., T.W. Britt, C.A. Castro, D. McGurk, and P.D. Bliese. (2011b). Effect of transition home from combat on risk-taking and health-related behaviors. *Journal of Traumatic Stress,* 24(4):381-389.

Algoe, S.B., and B.L Fredrickson. (2011). Emotional fitness and the movement of affective science from lab to field. *American Psychologist,* 66(1):35-42.

Bargh, J.A., and T.L. Chartrand. (1999). The unbearable automaticity of being. *American Psychologist,* 54(7):462-479.

Becker, C.M. (2004). Organizational routines: A review of the literature. *Industrial and Corporate Change,* 13(4):643-678.

Bower, G.H., and J.P. Forgas. (2000). Affect, memory, and social cognition. In E. Eich, J.F. Kihlstrom, G.H. Bower, J.P. Forgas, and P.M. Niedenthal, Eds., *Cognition and Emotion* (pp. 87-168). New York: Oxford University Press.

Cacioppo, J.T., H.T. Reis, and A.J. Zautra. (2011). Social resilience: The value of social fitness with an application to the military. *The American Psychologist,* 66(1):43-51.

Clapp-Smith, R., G.R. Vogelgesang, and J.B. Avey. (2009). Authentic leadership and positive psychological capital: The mediating role of trust at the group level of analysis. *Journal of Leadership and Organizational Studies,* 15(3):227-240.

Cornum, R., M.D. Matthews, and M.E.P Seligman. (2011). Comprehensive Soldier Fitness: Building resilience in a challenging institutional context. *The American Psychologist,* 66(1):4-9.

Cyert, R.M., and J.G. March. (1963). *A Behavioral Theory of the Firm.* Englewood Cliffs, NJ: Prentice-Hall.

Department of the Army. (2011). *Military Operations: Army Force Generation.* Army Regulation 525-29. Washington, DC: Headquarters, Department of the Army. Available: http://www.forscom.army.mil/graphics/r525_29.pdf [April 2014].

Duckworth, A.L., C. Peterson, M.D. Matthews, and D.R. Kelly. (2007). Grit: Perseverance and passion for long-term goals. *Journal of Personality and Social Psychology,* 92(6):1,087-1,101.

Eidelman, S., and C.S. Crandall. (2012). Bias in favor of the status quo. *Social and Personality Psychology Compass,* 6(3):270-281.

Feldman, M.S., and B.T. Pentland. (2003). Reconceptualizing organizational routines as a source of flexibility and change. *Administrative Science Quarterly,* 48(1):94-118.

Fraser, M.W. (1997). *Risk and Resilience in Childhood: An Ecological Perspective.* Washington, DC: NASW Press.

Fredrickson, B.L. (2003). The value of positive emotions: The emerging science of positive psychology is coming to understand why it's good to feel good. *American Scientist,* 91(4):330-335.

Gigerenzer, G., and D.G. Goldstein. (1996). Reasoning the fast and frugal way: Models of bounded rationality. *Psychological Review,* 103(4):650-669.

Gilligan, R. (2001). *Promoting Resilience: A Resource Guide on Working with Children in the Care System.* London, UK: British Agencies for Adoption and Fostering.

Grant, R.M. (1996). Toward a knowledge-based theory of the firm. *Strategic Management Journal,* 17:109-122.

Kahneman, D. (2003). Maps of bounded rationality: Psychology for behavioral economics. *American Economic Review,* 93(5):1,449-1,475.

Kahneman, D., and D.T. Miller. (1986). Norm theory: Comparing reality to its alternatives. *Psychological Review,* 93(2):136-153.

Kahneman, D., and A. Tversky. (1979). Prospect theory: An analysis of decision under risk. *Econometrica,* 47(2):263-292.

Kahneman, D., P. Slovic, and A. Tversky, Eds. (1982). *Judgment Under Uncertainty: Heuristics and Biases.* Cambridge, UK: Cambridge University Press.

Kline, A., M. Falca-Dodson, B. Sussner, D.S. Ciccone, H. Chandler, L. Callahan, and M. Losonczy. (2010). Effects of repeated deployment to Iraq and Afghanistan on the health of New Jersey Army National Guard troops: Implications for military readiness. *American Journal of Public Health,* 100(2):276-283.

Lant, T.K. (1992). Aspiration level adaptation: An empirical exploration. *Management Science,* 38(5):623-644.

Levinthal, D., and J.G. March. (1981). A model of adaptive organizational search. *Journal of Economic Behavior and Organization,* 2(4):307-333.

Luthans, F., B.J. Avolio, J.B. Avey, and S.M. Norman. (2007). Positive psychological capital: Measurement and relationship with performance and satisfaction. *Personnel Psychology,* 60(3):541-572.

Luthar, S.S., D. Cicchetti, and B. Becker. (2000). The construct of resilience: A critical evaluation and guidelines for future work. *Child Development,* 71(3):543-562.

March, J.G. (1981). Footnotes to organizational change. *Administrative Science Quarterly,* 26(4):563-577.

March, J.G., and H.A. Simon. (1958). *Organizations.* Cambridge, MA: Blackwell.

Meredith, L.S., C.D. Sherbourne, S.J. Gaillot, L. Hansell, H.V. Ritschard, A.M. Parker, and G. Wrenn. (2011). *Promoting Psychological Resilience in the U.S. Military.* Washington, DC: RAND Corporation. Available: http://www.rand.org/pubs/monographs/MG996.html [March 2014].

National Research Council. (2008a). *Human Behavior in Military Contexts.* Committee on Opportunities in Basic Research in the Behavioral and Social Sciences for the U.S. Military. J.J. Blascovich and C.R. Hartel, Eds. Board on Behavioral, Cognitive, and Sensory Sciences, Division of Behavioral and Social Sciences and Education. Washington, DC: The National Academies Press.

National Research Council. (2008b). *Behavioral Modeling and Simulation: From Individuals to Societies.* Committee on Organizational Modeling: From Individuals to Societies. G.L. Zachatias, J. MacMillan, and S. Van Hemel, Eds. Board on Behavioral, Cognitive, and Sensory Sciences, Division of Behavioral and Social Sciences and Education. Washington, DC: The National Academies Press.

Nelson, R.R., and S.G. Winter. (1982). *An Evolutionary Theory of Economic Change.* Cambridge, MA: Belknap Press of Harvard University Press.

Park, N. (2012). Adversity, resilience, and thriving: A positive psychology perspective on research and practices. In R.A. McMackin, E. Newman, J.M. Fogler, and T.M. Keane, Eds., *Trauma Therapy in Context: The Science and Craft of Evidence-Based Practice* (pp. 121-140). Washington, DC: American Psychological Association.

Peterson, C. (2006). *A Primer in Positive Psychology.* New York: Oxford University Press.

Peterson, C., N. Park, and C.A. Castro. (2011). Assessment for the U.S. Army Comprehensive Soldier Fitness program: The Global Assessment Tool. *American Psychologist,* 66(1):10-18.

Phillips, J., K. Quinn, R. Jaworski, M.C. Clouser, and M.R. Galarneau. (2013). *USMC Infantry Battalion Battle Injuries During an Operation Enduring Freedom (OEF) Deployment.* Paper presented at the Military Health System Research Symposium, Fort Lauderdale, FL. Symposium website available: http://mhsrs.amedd.army.mil/Pages/About-MHSRS.aspx [June 2014].

Pincus, S.H., R. House, J. Christenson, and L.E. Adler. (2001). The emotional cycle of deployment: A military family perspective. *U.S. Army Medical Department Journal,* 4(5):15-23.

Plank, T., S. Scheff, and A. Sebok. (2010). Capturing insights to reduce future warfighter fatalities. *Proceedings of the Human Factors and Ergonomics Society Annual Meeting,* 54(27):2,299-2,303.

Samuelson, W., and R. Zeckhauser. (1988). Status quo bias in decision making. *Journal of Risk and Uncertainty,* 1(1):7-59.

Seccombe, K. (2002). "Beating the odds" versus "changing the odds": Poverty, resilience, and family policy. *Journal of Marriage and Family,* 64(2):384-394.

Simon, H.A. (1982). *Models of Bounded Rationality: Empirically Grounded Economic Reason,* Vol. 3. Cambridge, MA: MIT Press.

Verplanken, B., I. Walker, A. Davis, and M. Jurasek. (2008). Context change and travel mode choice: Combining the habit discontinuity and self-activation hypotheses. *Journal of Environmental Psychology,* 28(2):121-127.

Walumbwa, F.O., F. Luthans, J.B. Avey, and A. Oke. (2011). Authentically leading groups: The mediating role of collective psychological capital and trust. *Journal of Organizational Behavior,* 32(1):4-24.

Winter, S.G. (1964). Economic "natural selection" and the theory of the firm. *Yale Economic Essays,* 4(1):225-272.

Wood, W., L. Tam, and M.G. Witt. (2005). Changing circumstances, disrupting habits. *Journal of Personality and Social Psychology,* 88(6):918-933.

4

Contextual Leadership

The Army has a long track record of developing and implementing leadership training, process, and policy, much of which the committee finds to be effective at cultivating good leaders into better leaders. The committee therefore believes that future research on leadership, while continuing to pursue modest benefits of incremental improvements to existing well-developed programs, should be expanded to include research on the role of social interactions in creating the social context for desirable individual behavior and small unit performance (Zaccaro et al., 2002). In this chapter, social interactions are defined as behaviors and actions of the individuals within a small unit; these interactions are the foundation for the social context of the unit that includes attitudes, feelings, and meaning attached to those interactions. Important social interactions of a small unit are not limited to those between unit members or to the influence of leaders upon unit members; the social context of a small unit is also defined by the mutually influencing interactions between leaders and followers, to include the influence followers have on their leaders.

While leaders of military small units should, first and foremost, "do no harm," the committee and the Army have higher expectations for the positive influence leaders can have on the individual and the unit. The committee believes that, over time, the fundamental understanding of social interactions within military units from the recommended research will position the Army to develop *contextual leaders* who effectively interpret, assess, and mold the social interactions within the unit to influence the desired social context, capitalize on opportunities as they evolve, and ultimately, enhance unit performance: the extent to which a unit successfully completes its assigned missions.

In this chapter, the committee develops a research agenda to answer three fundamental questions regarding contextual leadership:

1. What knowledge and skills do leaders require to understand and address social interactions within a unit?
2. What types of interactions exert the strongest influence, positively and negatively, on unit performance under differing environmental conditions?
3. How can leaders influence social interactions so as to have the most positive impact on unit performance?

To research these questions, the committee believes small units must be assessed longitudinally to understand how they morph and change as distinct groups and as a part of the larger organization. With a longitudinal approach, it will be possible to collect data relevant to unit membership and leader turnover as well as to the developing roles of women and other minority groups (e.g., race or ethnicity and sexual orientation) within various military environments. Ultimately, this research will provide a fundamental understanding of how leaders shape and mold social interactions to coordinate their followers on good behaviors. Consistent with this report's earlier discussion of norms (see Chapter 2), leaders communicate and amplify the organizations' desired behaviors, habits, and norms. Leaders contribute to group norms, and far more needs to be known about how they detect and influence these norms (Hogg and Terry, 2000).

STATE OF RESEARCH

Leadership has been extensively studied by scholars across different academic disciplines (e.g., anthropology, economics, evolutionary biology, history, industrial/organizational psychology, primatology, political and organizational science, and psychology), as well as in military-specific domains, espousing a variety of goals and perspectives.[1] At its core, leadership is about coordinating action by a group of individuals for some purpose, typically to reach a desired goal or end state (e.g., a unit's tactical mission). Leaders also "motivate people both inside and outside the chain

[1]For a more comprehensive review of leadership research, see recent publications that summarize this research either qualitatively (Kaiser et al., 2008; Yukl, 2012; Day, 2012; Day and Antonakis, 2012; Barling et al., 2010) or quantitatively with meta-analyses (Eagly and Johnson, 1990; Eagly et al., 1995; DeRue et al., 2011; Dirks and Ferrin, 2002; Burke et al., 2006; Bono and Judge, 2004; Judge and Piccolo, 2004; Judge et al., 2004b; Gerstner and Day, 1997; Ilies et al., 2007).

of command to pursue actions, focus thinking and shape decisions for the greater good of the organization" (Department of the Army, 2012a, p. 1). Consequently, leadership research seeks to understand the difference between leaders who successfully coordinate and motivate and those who do not.

Much of this research falls into one of two camps: (1) searching for leadership universals that apply broadly or (2) focusing on situational context as an important modifier for leadership antecedents and consequences. In military environments, perhaps more so than in some others, the situational context requires leaders to choose appropriate times to manage (or command) and to lead (especially by example, in the context of small units). Leaders of military small units may also be faced with huge responsibilities to accomplish the mission, with limited authority to implement organizational rewards or punishments on unit members—making military small unit leaders distinct from the leaders who are typically the subjects of research into successful leadership in big business or even small entrepreneurial endeavors. Furthermore, the committee cautions the Army against oversimplifying research conducted on business executives in order to apply conclusions from such research to leaders of Army small units. The relationships between leaders and followers in small units are distinct from those between business executives and employees of the corporate world, and insufficient research has been conducted on similar groups (with respect to size, responsibility, mission, etc.) to be of much utility to the Army. The existing research on leadership (outside military contexts) provides a basic foundation for future programs of military-relevant research, but it does not yet adequately answer all the important basic research questions relevant to satisfying the demands for good leadership within military environments.

Based on its review of the literature, the committee concludes that leadership is not exclusively about the leader. Extensive research to define good leadership through universal traits or attributes (e.g., Craig and Charters, 1925; Tead, 1935; Stogdill, 1948; Bird, 1940; House and Aditya, 1997; Richardson and Hanawalt, 1952; Bono and Judge, 2004) or through universal leader behaviors (Kerr et al., 1974; Judge and Piccolo, 2004; Judge et al., 2004a) have not convincingly shown that universalism, at least as defined in "universal trait" theories, is correlated with good performance (i.e., effective leaders). Decades of studies have failed to show consistent results, which may be due to methodological differences (Judge et al., 2004b), but may also be due to a fallacy inherent in the intuitive appeal of constructing a universal taxonomy of effective leader behaviors (e.g., Yukl, 2012). However, Day (2012) notes that recent advances in statistical analysis and other research methodologies have led to a renewed interest in leader traits.[2]

Despite the appeal of universal traits—those attributes such as character, presence, and intellect (Department of the Army, 2012a, 2012b) that make one leader superior to another—the committee believes the Army will find more utility in contingency-based and transformational theories of leadership, which demonstrate that there are different behaviors (or traits) that are more effective in different contexts and that leadership is more about the process than the person (e.g., Bass and Riggio, 2006; Day, 2012; Fiedler, 1967; Hanna et al., 2009; House, 1977; Kerr and Jermier, 1978). This research shows particular contextual parameters are most important: the complexity of the task at hand, the power or authority of the leader, the skills of the leader and the followers, cultural norms about what is appropriate behavior, and the relationship between the leader and follower. In the committee's judgment, effective leaders are those able to assess situations in the face of complexity and uncertainty and to adjust what they do to the situation and the needs of their followers—in short, effective leadership is context dependent.

The committee assesses that the search for universal traits to define effective leaders has not revealed any definitive answers; what is effective in one situation is not necessarily effective in another. What is not yet adequately understood is the importance and role of leadership in interpreting specific social interactions and creating the appropriate social context within the small military unit to foster conditions for success. Furthermore, most leadership attributes are studied in relatively stable contexts; the dynamic and shifting context of military environments provides unique challenges that must be studied more specifically.

LEADERSHIP IN THE ARMY

It should come as no surprise that the committee judges leadership to be an integral part of the success of the U.S. Army and broader military services, worthy of continued and expanded research efforts. Current Army doctrine asserts, "Leadership, the lifeblood of an army, makes a difference every day in the United States Army" (Department of the Army, 2012a, p. 1). Furthermore, the committee found the emphasis on leadership in Army doctrine to be well aligned with perspectives of representative service members with whom the committee met. During data-gathering sessions, active duty and former military service members representing a range of ranks,

[2]In this chapter, the committee refers to *leader traits*, a usage consistent with much of the historical research. However, we understand that Army doctrine now largely refers to *leader attributes*, which we consider, for purposes of this report, as synonymous with leader traits.

occupational specialties, and lengths of service repeatedly asserted that the Army's mission and organizational success rely heavily upon high-quality leadership.[3] The Army first published doctrine on leadership as a small pamphlet in 1948. From those brief words, the Army's concept of leadership as a process has evolved and expanded (see Department of the Army 2012a, 2012b), while retaining an underlying belief that leadership is a process that "can be learned, monitored and improved" (Department of the Army, 2012a, p. 1). The committee agrees and concludes that research into new and expanded facets of leadership will likely result in significant payoffs in achieving higher levels of organizational effectiveness, and thereby, mission success.

Accordingly, the Army's interest in basic research to understand leadership capabilities is not surprising. For decades, the U.S. Army Research Institute for the Behavioral and Social Sciences (ARI) has sponsored both in-house and outside research on leadership (e.g., see Butler et al., 1987). Currently, its Foundational Science Research Unit includes "Leader Development" as one of six primary research portfolios and goals (U.S. Army Research Institute for the Behavioral and Social Sciences, 2013). Its emphasis "is to advance theoretical understanding of leadership and leadership development . . . to create leader development methods for maximizing the requisite cognitive, perceptual, and interpersonal skills for effective leadership across all levels of command" (U.S. Army Research Institute for the Behavioral and Social Sciences, 2014, p. 31). While the committee recognizes that a great deal of high-quality research on leadership already exists and is ongoing in many distinct areas of academia, business, and military-specific environments, we conclude that there are significant potential areas of research that remain untapped.

One of the most important things the Army can gain from future research on leadership is a greater understanding of the nature and etiology of the verbal and nonverbal social interactions that distinguish leaders of effective military units from ineffective units, given the context of military environments. In its proposed research agenda, the committee emphasizes the importance of contextual leadership, a term derived from the concept of contextual intelligence (Mayo and Nohria, 2005). According to Mayo and Nohria's assessment of some of the 20th century's greatest leaders, those with high contextual intelligence are superbly able to understand an evolving environment and are able to capitalize on opportunities as they appear. For example, in business organizations there is a growing realization that

[3]The committee notes that it was unable to interview current junior enlisted soldiers through the course of this study, and although several of the interviewed commissioned and senior noncommissioned officers began their military careers as junior enlisted soldiers, that part of their military experience occurred some years previously.

leadership development must go beyond replicating observed behaviors of successful leaders, with the assumption that what works for a successful leader in one situation or set of conditions is applicable to all leaders in all situations and conditions (Kurtz, 2008; Mayo and Nohria, 2005; Nye, 2013). The National Research Council report, *Human Behavior in Military Contexts*, also asserted that "some leadership characteristics are more suited to some situations than others" (National Research Council, 2008). Similarly, Kaplan and Kaiser (2013) suggest that leaders who rely too heavily on a particular style or strength may be those least able to cope; their strengths may become their greatest problem. "Forcefulness can become bullying; decisiveness can turn into pigheadedness; niceness can develop into indecision" (*The Economist*, 2013).

Contextual leadership may, in many cases, be closely related to the Army's concept of situational leadership in which "leaders adjust their actions based on the situation," which "influences what purpose and direction are needed" (Department of the Army, 2012a, p. 4). The Army describes the situation as "the setting, the people and team, the adversary, cultural and historical background, and the mission to be accomplished" (Department of the Army, 2012a, p. 4). However, the idea of contextual leadership takes a broader perspective by including more-complex social and organization factors that are missing from the Army's characterization of situations, such as social interactions and organizational policy. The committee focuses on contextual leadership, because, consistent with our charge, we believe that future research must allow for greater inclusion of those social and organizational factors, especially social interactions, that contribute to the social context within which leaders operate.

FUTURE RESEARCH ON CONTEXTUAL LEADERSHIP

The committee believes that understanding social interactions of unit members and the evolving social context of the unit is critical to the development of effective contextual leadership in military environments. Leaders must "[foster] a command climate that challenges people, convinces them that their contributions make a difference, and allows them to feel good about themselves and the Army they serve. We have to take the time to see, hear, and resolve problems before they affect our units and our soldiers" (Rush, 2010, p. 5).

Conclusion 4

The committee concludes that leaders play a critical role in influencing the social context, which in turn shapes positive individual behavior and effective unit performance. Understanding the social interaction of unit members and the evolving social context of the unit, to include the mutually influencing relationship between leaders and followers, is critical to effective contextual leadership in military environments.

Recommendation 4
The U.S. Army Research Institute for the Behavioral and Social Sciences and other U.S. military funding agencies should fund an agenda of basic research to identify:

1. **specific challenges to leadership created by dynamic units and systems of units over time;**
2. **leadership capabilities that support soldier adjustment to military service;**
3. **the early warning signals of undesirable behaviors and appropriate counter measures; and**
4. **how leaders can influence social interactions so as to have the most positive impact on unit performance.**

Contextual Leadership Research Topics

The judgment underlying the recommended research agenda is that the leader plays a critical role in influencing the social context that leads to positive individual behavior and effective unit performance. To be effective, a leader must interpret, assess, and mold the social interactions within the unit to attain the desired social context. In the future, results from basic research on social interactions can assist the Army in addressing challenges and opportunities of contextual leadership in four areas: leaders of continually morphing units; managing expectations, reality, and motivation; early indicators of undesirable individual behaviors; and leadership influence on social interactions.

Leaders of Continually Morphing Units

A fundamental concern of military operations is that units must be kept up to strength, especially during overseas deployments during times of conflict. Organizational policies to satisfy the operational need for personnel, including rotating and replacing individuals versus replacing entire units, have been widely debated (e.g., Gabriel and Savage, 1978; Rush, 2001; see also Chapter 3). Currently, the Army Force Generation directive (Department of the Army, 2011) specifies a core process for force generation for both active Army and reserve components in an attempt to provide a sustained flow of forces for current commitments and unexpected contingencies based on a 3-year cycle of training, deployment, and recovery.

Regardless of any specific organizational policy, however, continually morphing units are a constant reality of military environments that impact the social interactions and resulting social context of the unit. Through conversations with military service members, the committee understands that challenges to leaders of morphing units are especially compounded when those units include soldiers who are scheduled for some type of administrative discharge or who have elected not to reenlist but who may remain in their units for over a year. However, the expected and unexpected entrance and exit of personnel to and from work groups is not unique to military environments and creates a social context worth understanding more fully. Relevant and important research questions for these considerations included the following:

- What distinct leadership behaviors facilitate and encourage rapid and lasting assimilation of replacement individuals and units such that a desired social context is maintained or enhanced (including, for example, desirable interactions, cohesion, and trust)?
- How can replacement individuals, who change the dynamics of the small unit, be encouraged to strengthen the group (invigorate with fresh ideas; rethink outdated practices, etc.)?
- What organizational structures may encourage new unit members to question and report unethical or illegal conduct, when it exists? What organizational structures may encourage and facilitate leaders to resolve such behaviors (or vice versa, discourage action from leaders)?
- How does trust evolve in a unit with rotating individual members? At what points might an effective leader have the most influence over this evolution?
- What social interactions should leaders attend to as units morph? What is the role of contextual leadership in ensuring that unit composition maximizes unit operational effectiveness? What techniques and tools are required for effective leadership under continually morphing conditions of diversity?

Managing Expectations, Reality, and Motivation

While potentially attractive to certain recruits, the readily available montage of official and unofficial media materials, which may promote expectations of becoming a "universal soldier," simultaneously risk creating a substantial dissonance between expectations and reality of military service. Combined data from a 2010 and 2011 survey of military veterans indicate that among living veterans from any era (including both World Wars, Vietnam, and Korea), approximately 15 percent of women and 35 percent of men have served in a combat or war zone (Patten and Parker,

2011). Those who serve in military combat roles are typically few compared to those who spend their days working in noncombat environments ranging from mechanical warehouses to high-rise offices. "The Army says that about 200,000 of its 1.1 million jobs are either direct combat or related jobs such as field artillery, combat engineers and so on. That's roughly 20 percent of the force, though the direct-combat front-line fighters make up roughly half of that or about 9 percent" (Baldor, 2014). The dissonance between expectations and reality is not unique to the military environment, and many industries struggle with similar challenges of managing expectations (see, for example, Elliot et al., 2009; Halfer and Graf, 2006; Harvey et al., 2012; Murray et al., 2011) and motivating employees (see, for example, Bartol and Locke, 2000; Chao et al., 1994). The following are examples of research questions pertinent to managing expectations:

- What are the most effective tactics to manage expectations of new unit members when expectations are inconsistent with reality?
- How can a leader effectively motivate performance of unit members who are disillusioned by the realities of military service (to include, for example, job duties, career path, deployments, etc.)? How can a leader help soldiers feel part of the Army mission when they are far removed from the military operations they may have signed on to experience?

Early Indicators of Undesirable Individual Behaviors

Effective small unit performance is a function of the combined effect of the behaviors of individual unit members, to include leaders and those they lead. These behaviors take place both before and during defined missions, in the security of a home base and in the stress of forward combat environments, and in ways that may not always have a directly apparent relationship to the performance of mission-related tasks. Behaviors of concern (e.g., discrimination, high-risk behaviors, abuse of alcohol or drugs, hazing, and sexual harassment and assault) jeopardize unit members' contributions to unit effectiveness. Undesirable behaviors may be present in small unit leaders and members alike, and Chapter 5 discusses the impact of misalignments in power and status that may lead to undesirable behaviors.

Furthermore, severe acts, like attempted suicide, have devastating and lasting repercussions for the individual soldier, the unit, and the Army as a whole. Behaviors of concern affect both those who exhibit them and those who are exposed to them, including targets of aggressive behavior. These effects can extend beyond the military ranks to include violations of the code of conduct of soldiers against civilians and helpless enemy combatants (including those imprisoned). Though rare in occurrence, such behaviors have occurred in multiple conflicts in American history, and their impact can be disastrous.[4] Furthermore, when subsequent decisions are made up the chain of command to protect those involved, it comes at the expense of victims and the U.S. military mission as well as American international political status (e.g., slow reactions to allegations such as mistreatment of detainees [Korb and Halpin, 2004] or intentional civilian killings [Voice of America, 2011]).

Of course, many of these behaviors are not unique to military service members and may be the result of internal personal struggles; however, military environments may create unique external stressors that may exacerbate tendencies toward these or other undesirable behaviors. The level of "moral character and moral courage" within the military comes with great consequences, and understanding the fundamental behavioral phenomena at play is critical before any policy or procedure can be expected to incite change.[5] Therefore, the committee proposes developing a fundamental understanding of the basic types of social interactions that indicate to leaders when internal and external stressors threaten to overload individual control and to aid leaders in assessing and intervening in potentially harmful situations. In the case of violent attacks, for example, emerging research indicates that well-defined early indicators (or warning behaviors) exist that "are dynamic and acute behaviors that precede an act of targeted violence, are related to it, and are therefore a risk factor for it" (National Research Council, 2011, p. 80).

The committee cautions that the lessons distilled from the research results on undesirable individual behaviors must be communicated to those in leadership positions in such a way as to facilitate appropriate implementation. A particular concern is to avoid delivering just enough knowledge, without adequate understanding, that the information on warning behaviors becomes likely to be used inappropriately, with potentially negative repercussions for individual unit members and entire units. These issues about dealing with undesirable behaviors may be addressed by the following research questions (among others):

- What categories of social interactions have the greatest influence on the social context of the unit (i.e., the types of interactions leaders should pay the greatest attention to forestalling, if their influence is negative, or to promoting, if their influence is positive)?

[4]For discussion of such occurrences, see "5 major atrocities in US military history." Global Post, March 12, 2012. Available: http://www.globalpost.com/dispatch/news/war/military/120312/major-atrocities-us-military-history [December 2013].

[5]And concerning moral and ethical lapses occurring recently across the services, the growing problem has already drawn the attention of Defense Secretary Hagel [New York Times, 2014].

- What are the early indicators of behavioral creep from mildly inappropriate or counterproductive actions to serious offenses?
- What contextual factors are important in determining the perception and impact of behaviors across different contexts (for instance, when the same behavior becomes problematic as contexts change)?
- What mechanisms encourage individuals (soldiers, including small unit leaders and unit members) to live by an ethical code (specifically, the Army's ethical code)?
- What are the most effective techniques that leaders of small units can employ to assess the changing social context of their units so as to diagnose and resolve problems at the earliest point possible to ensure the highest levels of unit performance?
- What categories of social interactions might indicate the presence of a toxic leader?
- What organizational factors may drive some of the behaviors associated with toxic leadership?
- What organizational factors may empower leaders to take action to remove unsuitable subordinate leaders from their positions or from the organization entirely?
- Is education and training alone enough to reduce or eliminate destructive leadership?

Leadership Influence on Social Interactions

One example of how the Army might consider the ability of leaders to influence social interactions within their small unit, and consequently of the social context unit members experience, is to seek to understand the influence of representative diversity of leaders and those they lead on small unit functioning. In many ways, the U.S. military can boast of a tremendously positive record of integrating female and racial minority soldiers and leaders, commemorating, in 2008, 60 years of integration within the armed forces (Carden, 2008). However, in others ways, the military has been slow to establish full integration of women (e.g., the 2013 reversal of the 1994 ruling that prohibited female soldiers from assignment to "military units and positions which may require engagement in direct combat" [Congressional Record, 1994]). In 2012, the "total" Army (including active duty, reserves, and national guard) was composed of 15.7 percent females (Department of Defense, 2012) and 39 percent racial/ethnic minorities.[6] When these members of the Army workforce are not utilized to their fullest

---

[6]Statistics obtained from FY12 Army Profile. Army G-1, Office of Army Demographics, FY12 Army Profile, provided to committee during its April 30, 2013 meeting. Document available by request through this study's public access file.

potential, the efficiency and effectiveness of the organization as a whole suffers, making organizational opportunities for women and minority leaders not only an issue of social concern but also one of organizational human resource management.

However, it is inappropriate to expect leaders to be uniform across gender and ethnic or racial lines. In fact, research shows that female and minority leaders display different strengths and are thereby perceived differently within different contexts (see Chapter 5). While studies conducted outside military environments (e.g., Eagly and Johnson, 1990; Eagly et al., 1995) suggest it is important for leaders of small units, especially female and other minority leaders, to understand how they are perceived by their unit, the impact of specific factors relevant only in military environments is not adequately understood (e.g., the impact of rank, Army demographics, increased opportunities for women in combat roles). Consequently, it is critical that further research in this area be conducted to understand how these factors affect real soldiers in real military environments.

Several aspects about the Army struck the committee as being particularly indicative of the need for research along these lines, especially at the small unit level. For example, responding to a 2009 congressional mandate, the Military Leadership Diversity Commission conducted a comprehensive study of leadership diversity in the U.S. military (Military Leadership Diversity Commission, 2011). In its report, the commission presents data on minorities (including racial and ethnic minorities and women) across the services that demonstrate important differences in minority representation between officer and enlisted service members, junior and senior ranks, and broad occupational specialties. While the report compares aggregate military diversity data with subgroups to show insightful cases of underrepresentation and overrepresentation, the level of analysis remains insufficient to be of much utility in understanding the social context of small units. In reviewing this report and other Army demographic and diversity data, the committee noted that the existing research assesses broad diversity trends in the Army (and other services) as a whole, with the lowest level of breakdown being the division between junior (E-1 to E-6 and O-1 to O-6) and senior (E-7 to E-9 and general officers) enlisted and officer ranks. Furthermore, the committee finds that the broad approach to tracking diversity across the entire Army has resulted in gaps of understanding in important details of diversity distribution across the Army branches, and more specifically among the occupational specialties. An effective diversity program cannot be implemented without a fundamental understanding of the Army branches and occupations where minority members and leaders may be overrepresented or underrepresented (for example, minorities are not underrepresented in functional support and administrative occupations; Military Leadership Diversity Commission, 2011), as well as an understanding of the social and organizational factors that might influence the distribution.

Therefore, the committee emphasizes the need to collect and assess diversity data on small unit members and leaders, including their Military Occupational Specialty and assigned company/platoon/detachment type. Data with this level of detail will likely enable organizational mechanisms to help leaders, especially female and minority leaders, understand how to influence social interactions at the small unit level within dynamic and evolving social contexts of military environments.

- How does service members' social identity relate to their leadership potential, and where can these be leveraged to successfully introduce female or other minority leaders?
- What values and norms can be used by minority leaders to demonstrate that they embody the qualities of idealized leaders (such as courage and service to others)?

A Research Approach

This section presents several research approaches (separated into sequential phases) the committee believes could benefit ARI and other U.S. funding agencies in developing a research program on contextual leadership. First and foremost, the proposed research agenda requires an integrated approach, which may begin with nonmilitary populations but must develop access to soldiers assigned to small units in order to obtain descriptions of the full range of social interactions that take place in military environments. Moreover, the needed data are not likely to be obtainable through simple observation; the interpretation, significance, emotional content, and urgency of each interaction must be collected via communication with the individuals. Consequently, while observation of interactions among unit members may be one source of data, these data must be augmented by information obtained on the associated cognitive and emotional processes within the individual unit members, which are not directly observable as overt behaviors and so require self-reporting, interviewing, and other established methods of indirect observation. As emphasized throughout this report, careful attention should be paid in designing these research programs so as not to overburden the force or individual soldiers with repetitive surveys but rather to capture their experiences and observations in a manner conducive to learning from their valuable input.

Furthermore, the issue of accurate measurements of leadership quality and effectiveness is a challenge that constrains the utility of the existing research. While achievements of formal rank, receipt of military awards and decorations, performance appraisals, and surveys provide useful information, it will be important to investigate contextual leadership through broader means to better understand the qualitative (and more subjective) aspects of leadership within the context of social interactions. Several possibilities—including field observations and unobtrusive data collection devices—are discussed below.

Many of the questions the committee has raised are enduring and fundamental. But there are opportunities for innovations in research, partly based on recent technological advances in telemetered recording of social interactions (Greene, 2008). First, an aggressive focus should develop measures of effective leadership at the level of the small unit. How can these new technologies be used to provide discriminating assessments of (1) leaders' (e.g., lieutenants and sergeants) abilities to communicate objectives to soldiers at every level below them (in other words, how well do the lowest privates understand the "Commander's Intent"?), and (2) leaders' situation awareness of the skills and motivation levels of the individual soldiers serving under them? Second, opportunities should be explored to utilize high-tech telemetering devices (e.g., smart badges or research-drone-based observation stations) to provide a much more complete record of moment-to-moment interactions of all members of a small unit (Hollingshead and Poole, 2012). Finally, the data from these sources should be analyzed using new analytic and modeling methods to derive a more discerning image of the daily social networks and social experiences of members of Army small units.

The committee suggests that ARI consider implementing this initial research effort in four phases, as described below.

Phase 1: Review of Survey Data

The Department of Defense has been operating a large-scale longitudinal study since 2001, the Millennium Cohort Study.[7] While the data collected in that study, in its current form, do not appear to provide information relevant to the recommended study of social interactions and social context and, more specifically, of contextual leadership, one of the recommendations of this report is to develop a longitudinal survey designed to collect the data necessary to address some of these issues (see Chapter 7). In doing so, it may be possible to obtain some broad background information on the awareness, understanding, and nature of social interactions in military units.

---

[7]Programmatic information on the Millennium Cohort Study is available at http://www.millenniumcohort.org/ [March 2014].

Phase 2: Exploratory Data Collection

This phase consists of unstructured data collection by means of observations and interviews. The objective is to capture, to the extent possible, the full range of the types of social interactions that take place in small units in three environments of interest (as emphasized to the committee by ARI and which include wide variations across spectrums of variables such as threat level, operational tempo, and duration): deployed outside the wire, deployed on a military installation, and at home station (inside and outside the United States). Observations would be made in a variety of environments, including, for example, day-to-day garrison routines and stressful training exercises, with a focus on identifying and documenting the social interactions observed. Interviews would be conducted with small unit members and leaders and with leaders with command responsibility for the participating units (likely a lieutenant or captain and their non-commissioned officer counterparts, the platoon sergeant or first sergeant). The product of this effort will be a preliminary listing and description of social interactions along with some initial insight as to their impact on the social context within small units in the context of that particular military environment. These data will serve to guide the design of data collection approaches, methods, and instruments to be employed in Phase 3.

Phase 3: Data Collection during Training Exercises

The third phase consists of systematic, structured data collection from a sample of military units during stressful graded training exercises, such as at the Joint Readiness Training Center and National Training Center. Data collection instruments will be tailored to reflect the nature and objectives of the training exercises and to obtain detailed descriptions of the social interactions that take place. Technology is now available in the form of wearable data collection devices, such as smart watches and headsets, to minimize the intrusion of the data collection process. In addition, tools are under development (Miller and Rye, 2012) that can be employed for automatically analyzing data collected from interactions to assess dimensions of unit social context. Data collected will reflect, in detail along a timeline, the impact of specific interactions on the social context that existed within the unit during each exercise. Data collected on social interactions and social context will be related to measures and observations of unit performance.

Phase 4: Simulation Experiments

The final phase assumes that, in the near future, sufficient technical advances will be achieved in modeling and simulating small unit operations to provide a basis for conducting controlled experiments. For example, currently available agent-based modeling and adaptive-system simulation should be adaptable to conduct the required type of experiments. Experiments conducted through highly realistic simulations of military environments would permit tightly controlled studies to test a number of hypotheses developed in Phase 3 about the relative influence of types of social interactions on social context, the most effective ways in which desired and effective social interactions can be influenced by leadership actions, characteristics (especially social interactions) that are most likely to lead to negative and positive individual behaviors and unit dynamics in a particular military context, and the relative impact of various individual behaviors on unit performance and effectiveness. These results are expected to provide implications for leadership training, as well as possibly for leader selection and promotion.

REFERENCES

Baldor, L.C. (2014). AP Exclusive: Few Army Women Want Combat Jobs. Available: http://bigstory.ap.org/article/ap-exclusive-few-army-women-want-combat-jobs [March 2014].

Barling, J.A., A. Christie, and A. Hoption. (2010). Leadership. In S. Zedeck, Ed., *APA Handbook of Industrial and Organizational Psychology* (pp. 183-240). Washington, DC: American Psychological Association.

Bartol, K.M., and E.A. Locke. (2000). Incentives and motivation. In S.L. Rynes and B. Gerhard, Eds., *Compensation in Organizations: Current Research and Practice* (pp. 104-147). San Francisco, CA: Jossey-Bass.

Bass, B.M., and R.E. Riggio. (2006). *Transformational Leadership*, 2nd ed. Mahwah, NJ: Lawrence Erlbaum Associates.

Bird, C. (1940). *Social Psychology*. New York: Appleton-Century.

Bono, J.E., and T.A. Judge. (2004). Personality and transformational and transactional leadership: A meta-analysis. *Journal of Applied Psychology,* 89(5):901-910.

Burke, C.S., K.C. Stagl, C. Klein, G.F. Goodwin, E. Salas, and S.M. Halpin. (2006). What type of leadership behaviors are functional in teams? A meta-analysis. *The Leadership Quarterly,* 17(3):288-307.

Butler, J.S., J.D. Blair, R.L. Phillips, and N. Schmitt. (1987). Framework for Research on Leadership, Cohesion, and Values. Technical Report 770. November 1987. Alexandria, VA: U.S. Army Research Institute for the Behavioral and Social Sciences.

Carden, M.J. (2008). Defense Department Commemorates 60 Years of Armed Forces Integration. *American Forces Press Service,* August 6. Available: http://www.defense.gov/news/NewsArticle.aspx?ID=50715 [February 2014].

Chao, G.T., A.M. O'Leary-Kelly, S. Wolf, H.J. Klein, and P.D. Gardner. (1994). Organizational socialization: Its content and consequences. *Journal of Applied Psychology,* 79(5):730-743.

Congressional Record. (1994). Congressional Record Volume 140, Number 141, Monday, October 3, 1994. Available: http://www.gpo.gov/fdsys/pkg/CREC-1994-10-03/html/CREC-1994-10-03-pt1-PgS36.htm [February 2014].

Craig, D.R., and W.W. Charters. (1925). *Personal Leadership in Industry.* New York: McGraw-Hill.

Day, D.V. (2012). Leadership. In S.W.J. Kozlowski, Ed., *The Oxford Handbook of Organizational Psychology*, Vol. 1 (pp. 696-732). New York: Oxford University Press.

Day, D.V., and J. Antonakis. (2012). *The Nature of Leadership*. Thousand Oaks, CA: Sage.

Department of the Army. (2011). *Army Regulation 525-29. Military Operations: Army Force Generation*. Washington, DC: Headquarters, Department of the Army. Available: http://armypubs.army.mil/epubs/pdf/r525_29.pdf [April 2014].

Department of the Army. (2012a). *Army Doctrine Publication (ADP) 6-22, Army Leadership*. Washington, DC: Headquarters, Department of the Army. Available: http://armypubs.army.mil/doctrine/DR_pubs/dr_a/pdf/adp6_22_new.pdf [March 2014].

Department of the Army. (2012b). *Army Doctrine Reference Publication (ADRP) 6-22. Army Leadership*. Washington, DC: Headquarters, Department of the Army. Available: http://armypubs.army.mil/doctrine/DR_pubs/dr_a/pdf/adrp6_22_new.pdf [March 2014].

Department of Defense. (2012). *2012 Demographics: Profile of the Military Community*. Office of the Deputy Assistant Secretary of Defense (Military Community and Family Policy). Available: http://www.armyg1.army.mil/hr/docs/demographics/FY12_ARMY_PROFILE.pdf [June 2014].

DeRue, D.S., J. Nahrgang, N. Wellman, and S.E. Humphrey. (2011). Trait and behavioral theories of leadership: An integration and meta-analytic test of their relative validity. *Personnel Psychology*, 64(1):7-52.

Dirks, K.T., and D.L. Ferrin. (2002). Trust in leadership: Meta-analytic findings and implications for research and practice. *Journal of Applied Psychology*, 87(4):611-628.

Eagly, A.H., and B.T. Johnson. (1990). Gender and leadership style: A meta-analysis. *Psychological Bulletin*, 108(2):233-256.

Eagly, A.H., S.J. Karau, and M.G. Makhijani. (1995). Gender and the effectiveness of leaders: A meta-analysis. *Psychological Bulletin*, 117(1):125-145.

The Economist. (2013). Too much of a good thing: Leaders need to learn to beware of their strengths. June 8. Available: http://www.economist.com/news/business/21578990-leaders-need-learn-beware-their-strengths-too-much-good-thing [April 2014].

Elliot, T., T. Bromley, A. Chur-Hansen, and C. Laurence. (2009). Expectations and experiences associated with rural GP placements. *Rural and Remote Health*, 9(4):1264. Available: http://www.ncbi.nlm.nih.gov/pubmed/19968448 [March 2014].

Fiedler, F.E. (1967). *A Theory of Leadership Effectiveness*. New York: McGraw-Hill.

Gabriel, R.A., and P.L. Savage. (1978). *Crisis in Command: Mismanagement in the Army*. New York: Hill and Wang.

Gerstner, C.R., and D.V. Day. (1997). Meta-analytic review of leader-member exchange theory: Correlates and construct issues. *Journal of Applied Psychology*, 82(6):827-844.

Greene, K. (2008). Smart badges track human behavior. *MIT Technology Review*, January 30. Available: http://www.technologyreview.com/news/409459/smart-badges-track-human-behavior/ [February 2014].

Halfer, D., and E. Graf. (2006). Graduate nurse perceptions of the work experience. *Nursing Economics*, 24(3):150-155.

Hanna, S.T., M. Uhl-Bien, B.J. Avolio, and F.L. Cavarretta. (2009). A framework for examining leadership in extreme contexts. *The Leadership Quarterly*, 20(6):897-919.

Harvey, M., M.R. Buckley, G. Richey, M. Moeller, and M. Novicevic. (2012). Aligning expatriate managers' expectations with complex global assignments. *Journal of Applied Social Psychology*, 42(12):3,026-3,050.

Hogg, M.A., and D.I. Terry. (2000). Social identity and self-categorization processes in organizational contexts. *Academy of Management Review*, 25(1):121-140.

Hollingshead, A.B., and M.S. Poole, Eds. (2012). *Research Methods for Studying Groups and Teams: A Guide to Approaches, Tools, and Technologies*. New York: Taylor and Francis.

House, R.J. (1977). A 1976 Theory of Charismatic Leadership. In J.G. Hunt and L.L. Larsen, Eds., *Leadership: The Cutting Edge a Symposium Held at Southern Illinois University, Carbondale, October 27-28, 1976* (pp. 189-207). Carbondale: Southern Illinois University Press.

House, R.J., and R.N. Aditya. (1997). The social scientific study of leadership: Quo vadis? *Journal of Management*, 23(3):409-473.

Ilies, R., J.D Nahrgang, and F.P. Morgeson. (2007). Leader-member exchange and citizenship behaviors: A meta-analysis. *Journal of Applied Psychology*, 92(1):269-277.

Judge, T.A., and R.F. Piccolo. (2004). Transformational and transactional leadership: A meta-analytic test of their relative validity. *Journal of Applied Psychology*, 89(5):755-768.

Judge, T.A., R.F. Piccolo, and R. Ilies. (2004a). The forgotten ones? The validity of consideration and initiating structure in leadership research. *Journal of Applied Psychology*, 89(1):36-51.

Judge, T.A., A. Colbert, and R. Ilies. (2004b). Intelligence and leadership: A quantitative review and test of theoretical propositions. *Journal of Applied Psychology*, 89(3):542-552.

Kaiser, R.B., R. Hogan, and S.B. Craig. (2008). Leadership and the fate of organizations. *American Psychologist*, 63:96-110.

Kaplan, R.E., and R.B. Kaiser. (2013). *Fear Your Strengths: What You Are Best At Could Be Your Biggest Problem.* San Francisco, CA: Berrett-Koehler Publishers.

Kerr, S., and J.M. Jermier. (1978). Substitutes for leadership: Their meaning and measurement. *Organizational Behavior and Human Performance*, 22(3):375-403.

Kerr, S., C.A. Schreisheim, C.J. Murphy, and R.M. Stodgill. (1974). Toward a contingency theory of leadership based upon the consideration and initiating structure literature. *Organizational Behavior and Human Performance*, 12(1):62-82.

Korb, L.J., and J. Halpin. (2004). Cover-Up of Abu Ghraib Torture Puts Troops at Risk. *Center for American Progress*, May 11. Available: http://www.americanprogress.org/issues/terrorism/news/2004/05/11/770/cover-up-of-abu-ghraib-torture-puts-troops-at-risk/ [February 2014].

Kurtz, M.R. (2008). Contextual intelligence: An emerging competency for global leaders. *Regent Global Business Review*, 2(2):5-9.

Mayo, A.J., and N. Nohria. (2005). *In Their Time: The Greatest Business Leaders of the Twentieth Century.* Boston, MA: Harvard Business Press Books.

Military Leadership Diversity Commission. (2011). *From Representation to Inclusion: Diversity Leadership for the 21st-Century Military.* Arlington, VA: Military Leadership Diversity Commission. Available: http://diversity.defense.gov/Portals/51/Documents/Special%20Feature/MLDC_Final_Report.pdf [February 2014].

Miller, C., and J. Rye. (2012). Power and politeness in interactions: ADMIRE—a tool for deriving the former from the latter. In *Proceedings of the ASE International Conference on Cyber Security: December 14-16 2012*, Washington, DC. Conference website available: http://asesite.com/conferences/cybersecurity/2012/ [June 2014].

Murray, K., P. Toulson, and S. Legg. (2011). Generational cohorts' expectations in the workplace: A study of New Zealanders. *Asia Pacific Journal of Human Resources*, 49(4):476-493.

National Research Council. (2008). *Human Behavior in Military Contexts.* Committee on Opportunities in Basic Research in the Behavioral and Social Sciences for the U.S. Military. J.J. Blascovich and C.R. Hartel, Eds., Board on Behavioral, Cognitive, and Sensory Sciences, Division of Behavioral and Social Sciences and Education. Washington, DC: The National Academies Press.

National Research Council. (2011). *Threatening Communications and Behavior: Perspectives on the Pursuit of Public Figures.* C. Chauvin, Ed., Board on Behavioral, Cognitive, and Sensory Sciences, Division of Behavioral and Social Sciences and Education. Washington, DC: The National Academies Press.

New York Times. (2014). Hagel orders urgent push for military ethics crackdown. February 6. Available: http://nypost.com/2014/02/06/hagel-orders-urgent-push-for-military-ethics-crackdown/ [April 2014].

Nye, J.S. (2013). Effective leaders need contextual intelligence and intuition. *The Daily Star.* June 14. Available: http://www.dailystar.com.lb/Opinion/Commentary/2013/Jun-14/220337-effective-leaders-need-contextual-intelligence-and-intuition.ashx#axzz2yJ0uBkn5 [April 2014].

Patten, E., and K. Parker. (2011). Women in the U.S. Military: Growing Share, Distinctive Profile. December 22, 2011. *Pew Research Social and Demographic Trends.* Available: http://www.pewsocialtrends.org/2011/12/22/women-in-the-u-s-military-growing-share-distinctive-profile/ [April 2014].

Richardson, H.M., and N.G. Hanawalt. (1952). Leadership as related to the Bernreuter personality measures: V. Leadership among adult women in social activities. *Journal of Social Psychology,* 36(2):141-153.

Rush, R.S. (2001). *Hell in Hurtgen Forest: The Ordeal and Triumph of an American Infantry Regiment.* Lawrence, KS: University Press of Kansas.

Rush, R.S. (2010). *NCO Guide.* 9th ed. Mechanicsburg, PA: Stackpole Books.

Stogdill, R.M. (1948). Personal factors associated with leadership: A survey of the literature. *Journal of Psychology,* 25:35-71.

Tead, O. (1935). *The Art of Leadership.* New York: McGraw-Hill.

U.S. Army Research Institute for the Behavioral and Social Sciences. (2014). *Foundational Research in Behavioral and Social Sciences: Marching Towards the Future. Special Report 73.* Washington, DC: Department of the Army.

Voice of America. (2011). US soldier goes on trial for civilian atrocities in Afghanistan. October 26. Available: http://www.voanews.com/content/us-soldier-goes-on-trial-for-civilian-atrocities-in-afghanistan-132746613/168149.html [April 2014].

Yukl, G. (2012). Effective leadership behavior: What we know and what questions need more attention. *Academy of Management Perspectives,* 26(4):66-85.

Zaccaro, S.J., A.L. Rittman, and M.A. Marks. (2002). Team leadership. *The Leadership Quarterly,* 12(4):451-483.

5

Distinct Sources of Power and Status in Diversified Army Units

Military organizations are distinctive in the visibility and rigidity of their formal power hierarchies and chain of command. Military ranks define an explicit, consistent, complete ordering of formal authority and power. Furthermore, the paths of promotion to higher levels of power in the Army are well defined; there are few detours to promotion outside the standard routes and no "external hires." But, as in every organization, there are also important informal and less explicit sources of respect, esteem, and social influence that determine an individual's placement on the status hierarchy, a hierarchy distinct but interrelated to the power hierarchy. In this chapter, the committee proposes research to understand soldiers' access to positions of social influence and authority not only in the formal, rank-based power hierarchy but also through informal, respect-based sources of status in the Army. The proposed research addresses questions such as the following:

- To the extent that soldiers derive status from their similarity to ideal or typical soldiers, where do valued identities originate and how do these socially shared beliefs change?
- How do changes in the skills that are required in military operations impact how soldiers achieve status?
- How does the attainment of status influence career development, particularly for individuals who do not match the stereotype of the prototypical soldier (for example, individuals who are minorities in terms of gender, race, or sexual orientation or who represent a

smaller and different job skill than the majority within the unit they serve)?

- What are the implications for leadership and authority for soldiers from traditionally disadvantaged groups, whose informal status may not align with their formal power?

An individual's position on the informal status hierarchy is based on social perceptions of competence (especially tactical and technical competence in military environments) and the value that the individual brings to the unit's collective tasks. These social perceptions are influenced both by ascribed individual characteristics, such as race and gender, and by achieved characteristics, such as technical skills and experience (Berger, 1977). Because social perceptions of competence systematically vary by ascribed and achieved characteristics, some individuals are disadvantaged in their opportunities to attain high-status positions of social influence and, therefore, are disadvantaged in their ability to lead authoritatively and effectively. This chapter focuses first on issues that have to do with differential opportunities to move up in informal status hierarchies and second on the leadership implications for soldiers whose positions on power and status hierarchies are misaligned (e.g., soldiers who possess a higher formal rank but who have relatively low status within the small unit context).

Achievement of high status in Army small units varies on numerous dimensions. This discussion focuses on three prominent status-conferring attributes: gender, combat versus noncombat assignments,[1] and formal designations of military rank. Within military environments, the institutionalized rank system influences a soldier's power and status. For simplicity, we refer to an individual's placement on the formal power hierarchy in terms of achieved military rank, to include recognition of power differentials between officer and enlisted ranks (i.e., the most junior officer outranks the most senior enlisted member of the military). Additionally, military rank is also a signal or indicator of status and therefore explains much of

[1]Army jobs are grouped into military occupational specialties (MOS) for enlisted soldiers and functional areas for officers that are further grouped into branches (e.g., ordnance corps, infantry, and military intelligence). Historically, soldiers belonged to units in one of three categories: combat arms, combat support, or combat support services. In 2008, the Army rescinded these terms and units are now described by warfighting functions (Department of the Army, 2008, p. D-3). However, the concept of "combat and noncombat soldiers" remained salient to service members who engaged in discussions with the committee regarding job and unit assignments, combat awards, and status among unit members. For the purpose of this chapter, the term combat soldier refers to those soldiers whose MOS and job assignment comes with the expectation of direct engagement with enemy forces, and the term noncombat soldier refers to those soldiers whose warfighting functions are historically associated with combat support and combat support service units.

the status variance between individual soldiers; however, rank is only one among many status-conferring attributes.

To understand the importance of informal status hierarchies to mission success, the committee highlights the example of integrating women soldiers into rewarding, equal-opportunity Army careers. Future research into gender as a status-conferring attribute should be of particular interest because of the current shift in roles for women in the U.S. military services (for a historical account, see National Women's Law Center, 2013). Gender is also an ascribed attribute (a trait beyond the individual's control), on which status is assigned, that is prominent in scientific research on sources of power and status. The greater the gender imbalance within an organization (ratio of males to females, such as in the Army), the more gender seems to matter (Eagly et al., 1995). We also highlight challenges of status achievement for soldiers in noncombat jobs because of the traditional importance of combat duty to status attainment in the Army. Nonetheless, the committee does not intend to restrict the focus of research that might follow our recommendations to female or noncombat personnel. The research we propose should explore many other socially significant ascribed (e.g., race, sexual orientation) and acquired (e.g., technical competence) characteristics and their relevance to status hierarchies within the Army context.

To illustrate the importance of this topic, consider the following example. A new lieutenant is assigned to a platoon midway through its deployment and needs to take command quickly. In all likelihood, the new platoon leader will turn to the platoon sergeant for assistance during the leadership transition period. However, if additional or different support is needed, how does the platoon leader identify the noncommissioned officer (NCO) he can rely on to have the right expertise and informal leadership skills? He may look for signals of competence, experience, and bravery. For example, visual representations of military qualifications (e.g., an NCO's badges—tabs or insignia patches worn on the soldier's uniform) serve as an immediately accessible indicator of expertise. He may also notice who among the NCOs is most respected and trusted by the rest of the troops. He may assess who comes closest to his image of the ideal soldier: strong, brave, stoic, and Ranger-certified.[2]

But the success of the unit may be impacted if the NCO who has the greatest potential to assist the platoon leader does not have the right tab, the right image, or the right friends. Due to biases that favor individuals who exemplify an ideal soldier prototype, it may be difficult for the platoon leader to identify the smartest, bravest, most adaptive, and most committed

[2]The details of this paragraph are drawn from interviews with military service members with relevant personal experiences. The conclusions may be subjective and impressionistic, but they are based upon experiences described to the committee separately by several individuals.

soldier if that soldier is a woman who did not complete a coveted certification course applicable for her branch of service (e.g., Ranger certification[3] among combat arms soldiers) or who lacks connections to her peers in the social network because she is quartered in a different barracks and misses many of the bonding experiences available to other (male) soldiers. The platoon's mission may suffer if the platoon leader overlooks the potential contributions of an outstanding candidate who does not fit the traditional image of the ideal soldier, and in turn, those soldiers who do not fit traditional stereotypes may be frustrated and demotivated.

Importantly, the committee notes that, although there is a *prima facie* case to expect that women and soldiers of both genders assigned to noncombat jobs (or perhaps those who have not experienced direct combat) may be disadvantaged compared to males or soldiers with combat experience, we do not start from the assumption that these attributes result in career disadvantages. Indeed, the well-defined and methodical promotion-based military career paths make it distinctively important to conduct research on the effects of such attributes on career trajectories within the military context. In contrast, research on civilian career paths is likely to be much less definitive because of the enormous variation in conditions, career roles, promotion opportunities, and standards for evaluation of contributions and success. We elaborate below on the Army's unique opportunity to study sources and consequences of social status.

STATUS HIERARCHIES

Social science research has a long history of studying social hierarchies in task groups such as Army units (e.g., Bales et al., 1951; French and Raven, 1959; Blau, 1970; Russell, 1938; Goffman, 1967). Recent research has distinguished between hierarchies based on access to and control over resources (also called "power" hierarchies), which include the formal rank hierarchy in the Army,[4] and socially constructed hierarchies of respect and esteem-based expectations of competence and contribution to group goals, often called "status" hierarchies (for reviews, see Magee and Galinsky, 2008; Correll and Ridgeway, 2006). Numerous benefits accrue to the indi-

---

[3]As of the writing of this report, the Army has not yet opened its Ranger school to women; however, the Army Chief of Staff, General Raymond Odierno, has indicated that the Army will not adjust physical standards for women as they are integrated into ground combat roles. Furthermore, scientific validation of current physical fitness standards is required by the Army's Soldier 2020 initiative.

[4]The committee notes that power may be attained through means other than formal rank because certain roles such as logistics or supplies control access to resources. In our research questions, however, we focus on formal rank and informal status because they are both hierarchically organized social resources.

viduals who attain high positions in both power and status hierarchies. While many of the advantages of having higher versus lower power are self-evident, recent research has documented less obvious psychological effects of experiencing high power. Specifically, high power is associated with an approach mindset that is characterized by attention to rewards, positive emotions, automatic cognition, and behavioral disinhibition (Keltner et al., 2003). Low power, in contrast, produces an inhibition mindset, which is characterized by attention to threats, negative emotions, systematic and controlled cognitions, and constrained behavior (Keltner et al., 2003). Research has also documented substantial benefits of having relatively higher status, including more opportunities to contribute to group tasks, more positive evaluations for the contributions made, and more influence in group processes and outcomes (Bales, 1958; Magee and Galinsky, 2008; Berger et al., 1980). Although people and cultures differ in the degree to which they endorse the concept of status hierarchies (for individual differences, see work on "social dominance orientation" such as Sidanius and Pratto, 1993; for cultural differences see work on "power distance" such as Hofstede, 1980; Schwartz, 1994), these social structures and the relative benefits of being higher versus lower in them exist universally (Bales, 1958; Tiedens et al., 2007; Gould, 2003; Mazur, 1973).

Informal Status Versus Formal Power

A critical distinction between power and status is that power is more a property of an individual (the resources a person controls), whereas status is more a property of a social collective (it only exists in the eyes of others, or to the extent that others grant it to a person) (Emerson, 1962; Magee and Galinsky, 2008; Goldhamer and Shils, 1939; Goffman, 1967). Power hierarchies may be institutionally established and endorsed, as is the rank hierarchy of the Army; however, status hierarchies emerge organically through social negotiations (Strauss, 1978; Strauss et al., 1963). Therefore, the criteria used to determine opportunities to attain power often differ from those used to determine opportunities to attain status. Different people (or types of people) may have more access to power than to status, and there are conditions under which power and status are not perfectly aligned (Fragale et al., 2011; Fiske et al., 2007), as discussed in further detail in the second section of this chapter.

Status in task group contexts is not just social popularity. Perceptions of status are based on expected performance, specifically competence and contribution to achieve group goals (Berger, 1977; Berger et al., 1972, 1974, 1986; Correll and Ridgeway, 2006). Although social network centrality is another correlate of high status, scholars generally consider centrality in task-related advice networks to be more important than status in friendship networks (e.g., Podolny, 2005; Podolny and Baron, 1997; DeKlepper et al., 2013).

Yet performance expectations are in large part socially constructed. People have stereotypes about the qualities and resources associated with categories of people with particular characteristics (Ridgeway, 1991; Ridgeway and Balkwell, 1997; Ridgeway et al., 1998; Ridgeway and Erickson, 2000). Although there are idiosyncratic attributes for which individuals may be awarded high status, there are also categorical attributes that are systematically associated with higher and lower performance expectations (as an initial impression, that may or may not be validated by actual performance) and, hence, status values.

Prior research shows that in many workplace contexts, women have lower status than men because of their lower expected performance (Kanter, 1977; Ickes and Knowles, 1982; Biernat et al., 1998; Carli and Eagly, 1999; Lucas, 2003; Heilman and Okimoto, 2007; Heilman et al., 2004). The more masculine the workplace domain, meaning the more it values strength and competitiveness, the more difficult it is for women to demonstrate competence (Heilman, 2012; Eagly et al., 1995) because of the perceived incongruence between the valued skills (strength, competitiveness) and stereotypes about women: for example, that women are, or should be, warm, communal, and supportive (Fiske et al., 2002).

The socially constructed nature of status also means that people invest substantial personal resources (e.g., money, effort, attention) to enhance their status in groups (Bendersky and Shah, 2012; Pettit et al., 2010; Huberman et al., 2004). For example, group members may proactively demonstrate their task competence (Bunderson, 2003; Berger et al., 1974; Cheng et al., 2013), act generously to the group (Ridgeway, 1982; Willer, 2009; Flynn et al., 2006; Hardy and Van Vugt, 2006), behave dominantly (Anderson and Kilduff, 2009; Ridgeway, 1987; Ridgeway and Diekema, 1989) or aggressively (Faris, 2012; Faris and Felmlee, 2011), speak powerfully (Fragale, 2006), or express overconfidence (Anderson et al., 2012). Ironically, the status rewards for these behaviors can vary for people with different status-valued attributes. For instance, women often experience punitive backlash when they behave in a dominant or aggressive manner (Amanatullah and Tinsley, 2013; Berdahl, 2007; Rudman et al., 2012) or fail to show active support for others (Amanatullah and Tinsley, 2013), and women receive especially high rewards (compared to those received by men) for being generous towards others (Ridgeway, 1982; Eagly and Karau, 2002; Eagly and Johnson, 1990).

Once established, performance expectations can create self-fulfilling prophecies. Those in higher-status positions are given more opportunities and support for performing well than are lower-status members of groups (Bales, 1958; Berger et al., 1980; Magee and Galinsky, 2008). Social order is most stable when both high-status and low-status actors recognize their positions and conform appropriately (Ridgeway and Berger, 1986; Sampson, 1963). At the extreme, expectations can undermine the performance of stereotyped group members. For example, stereotypes about African Americans' inferior intellectual capabilities can create self-fulfilling prophecies for African Americans' performance on intellective tasks (Steele and Aronson, 1995), due to anticipated evaluative threats; similar effects have been found for women in technical fields of study (Pronin et al., 2004; Beilock et al., 2007). These results are most evident when stereotypes are subconsciously activated, as conscious awareness of any subordinating stereotype can elicit stereotype reactance: the desire to prove the stereotype wrong (Kray and Thompson, 2005; Kray et al., 2001).

Are There Opportunity Differences in Military Environments?

Some of the most contentious questions in current research concern the nature and consequences of differential treatments of individual members of organizations as a function of their background characteristics including gender, race, religion, and sexual preferences (Williams and O'Reilly, 1998). There are many social facts that seem to imply differential treatment or subconscious prejudice against the members of certain classes of individuals in particular settings. People's implicit, or subconscious, associations between race, gender, and performance have been related to a wide variety of differential treatment (Biernat et al., 1998; Jost et al., 2002; Rudman and Kilianski, 2000). But it is difficult to reach definite conclusions about the causes of these differences, and there is a continuing debate about how much of these differential outcomes is "legitimate" in the sense that it stems from differential performance and not just expectations and prejudices against classes of individuals.

The committee believes military service offers a unique setting in which to study the role of personal attributes (gender, race, aptitudes, etc.) on career achievements and to possibly develop empirical support for more definite conclusions. In particular, the extreme standardization of the formal military ranks, the well-defined job descriptions, and the extensive replication of cases of similar career tracks up the orderly military promotion paths provide a setting in which variables of interest can be controlled and suggestive results can be tested through replication. Although causality is difficult to determine for behavioral and social outcomes, military environments provide a context in which we believe it possible to frame and test precise hypotheses about the contributions of personal characteristics (including "social capital" and physical endowments), attitudes and organizational culture, institutional factors (allocations of responsibilities, opportunities, and training), and distribution of individuals in roles in the past (e.g., women in combat roles or African Americans promoted to general officers) on current and future promotion patterns. We note the value of the longitudinal database recommended in Chapter 7 as one instrument with which to pursue such research.

One such important personal attribute to study is the role of gender. Women are a minority in the Army, representing approximately 13 percent of active duty personnel (Department of Defense, 2012), and until recently, women have been excluded from many positions intended for engagement in direct combat[5] (see Harrell et al., 2007, for further discussion). The culture of the Army—as reflected in the Seven Core Army Values: loyalty, duty, respect, selfless service, honor, integrity, and personal courage[6]—suggests that women and noncombat personnel might face more obstacles in demonstrating competence and achieving status. For example, one way in which soldiers display their "ideal soldier" credentials is through the badge (insignia or tab) system that communicates the location and nature of soldiers' training and military experiences and any special qualifications they have earned, such as Army Ranger certifications. As was explained to the committee by military service members, soldiers often look at each other's badges and visible physical attributes to initially establish a widely shared understanding of their status hierarchy, which is heavily driven by masculine-typed achievements (e.g., passing the extreme "strength-based" physical challenges of special services training) and combat experience. Competencies will be validated over time through shared experiences within the unit, but surface-level indicators, like badges and physique, offer initial legitimacy and contribute to the ease with which status can be achieved.

A second important attribute that confers status in military environments is combat and noncombat job assignments. A paper on Army teams prepared for the committee by Major Benjamin J. Tupper (U.S. Army National Guard)[7] explains the divide between "combat arms" units (infantry, armor, Special Forces, and field artillery) whose soldiers directly engage enemy forces and support units that provide combat soldiers with "beans and bullets." Soldiers assigned to combat arms units have a degree of status that is evident through such behaviors as referring to support soldiers by unflattering nicknames such as "marshmallow soldiers." Tupper explains, "Support troops normally remain on large bases, 'in the rear,' living comfortable lives with air conditioning and shopping and elaborate chow halls,

---

[5]Is it worth noting, however, that despite the current combat exclusion policy, females are assigned to units that have engaged in direct fire, such as military police and attack aviation, and have received valorous commendations for their performance in direct fire environments in both Iraq and Afghanistan.

[6]Descriptions of the Seven Core Army Values are available at http://www.army.mil/values/ [April 2014].

[7]Paper available by request from this study's public access file.

while their combat arms brethren are out eating dirt and getting shot at" (p. 24). In short, combat arms soldiers enjoy a superior status because of their embodiment of the idealized soldier values.

Military environments and military careers provide distinctively effective research settings in which to explore comparative hypotheses about differences between the perceptions and treatment of members of minority groups defined by various attributes, as well as differences between combat and noncombat soldiers. For example, a research study can measure precisely in what ways women's military careers are similar to and different from others' military careers. Given the traditional female stereotypes, as well as visible differences in physical characteristics, women may be perceived as less powerful physically and less "warrior-like" temperamentally than their male peers. For example, longitudinal research that was conducted during a 9-week Army officer's leadership training course found persistent and increasing sex-based stereotyping of female officer's lesser competence and leadership effectiveness than males' (Biernat et al., 1998). Moreover, under some conditions, female soldiers are objects of sexual desire for male soldiers (Department of Defense, 2013). Military women may also face challenges in gaining status working in culturally different environments in which American allies as well as American enemies may have expectations of women that differ significantly from those typical in American society. How do these expectations and characteristics play out in ways that are specific to gender discrimination? And how are these possible career achievement disadvantages comparable to, and different from, the expectations, behaviors, and treatment of male African American soldiers? Furthermore, do the measures the Army has taken in the past to reduce the obstacles arising from racial prejudice (at least on career paths from the bottom to the middle of military ranks) offer insights that could be applied to improve the prospects for female soldiers' careers?

Of course, there are exceptions to any generalization about a topic as broad as gender and career achievements. There must be cases, including in military contexts, where expectations about female soldiers and leaders may be advantageous, even for the most tangible outcomes of performance evaluations and promotions (cf. Eagly and Carli, 2003; Eagly and Johannesen-Schmidt, 2001). Furthermore, in some cases, women may find their status in culturally different environments to be advantageous for certain military missions (e.g., Afghan female engagement teams [International Security Assistance Force, 2011]). One important objective for research on gender and military careers would be to identify the military roles and career paths that are currently the most supportive of achievements by women and other minority soldiers.

Based on current trends in technology and military strategy, the committee anticipates future combat roles will include a greater variance of necessary physical power, whereby some roles will be more "indirect" and require lower levels of physical power and endurance but higher levels of cognitive skills and capacities such as vigilance, detection, and inference. Some modern technologies (e.g., drones and long-range artillery) facilitate combat unlikely to require the physical strength and training necessary for hand-to-hand fighting. Simultaneously, however, the operating environments experienced by other combat soldiers (e.g., especially those engaged in special forces and counterinsurgency operations) may present greater physical challenges as the soldiers maneuver urban environments in close contact with enemy forces among noncombatants. Consequently, the value of attributes that have traditionally been associated with the ideal soldier, such as physical strength (Department of the Army, 2011, 2012a) and aggressiveness, may expand to alter the image of the ideal soldier prototype. It is this expansion of the ideal soldier prototype that the committee believes will be an important issue to understand as it relates to the attainment of status within the small unit. Thus, another question arises: As the activities of engaging in combat change so that a wider range of personal attributes and roles become important for mission accomplishment, how will this impact how soldiers achieve status?

One example of how social perceptions have evolved in response to changes in combat operations during the wars of the past decade has been the creation of the Combat Action Badge (CAB), as described by Major Tupper:[8]

> However, the playing field of bragging rights has gradually been leveled during the recent operations in Iraq and Afghanistan. These conflicts, which lack defined front lines and are known best for the [improvised explosive device] IED-type attacks (as opposed to traditional unit on unit fighting), have served to weaken some of the anti-support troop bias among combat arms soldiers. Truck drivers, military police, and other support forces have regularly been in combat, which has begrudgingly earned them the respect of many of their combat arms peers.
>
> Another equalizer has been the recognition of the sacrifices being made by support troops in combat through the creation of the Combat Action Badge (CAB). Prior to 2005, the Combat Infantryman Badge was the only badge awarded as recognition of direct combat experience, and it was only issued to infantry soldiers. Since 2005, the CAB is ... [available to] non-infantry [and non-special forces] soldiers who have [been engaged by the enemy or who have personally engaged the enemy], allowing truck drivers and other assorted support soldiers to wear recognition that they too were involved in direct combat with the enemy.
>
> Creating the CAB, while momentarily alienating the infantry, ultimately serves the greater goal of honoring the sacrifices of all Army teams, regard-

[8]Paper available by request from this study's public access file.

> less of their position. Personally, when I see a soldier wearing a CAB, I feel a greater sense of camaraderie, as I know they too have experienced the challenges of life and death combat. This has fostered a greater sense of appreciation in my mind for support soldiers.

As with any organization, there will always be individuals who inappropriately receive merit awards, recognition, and promotion. If inappropriate rewards become widespread, however, it may delegitimize the value of the award across the organization. This reiterates a point made earlier that visible indicators of military expertise offer initial legitimacy and contribute to the ease with which status can be achieved, but unit members will confirm these qualities and characteristics in action.

Similar efforts to expand opportunities for women to enter all fields of operations in the Army, including the full spectrum of direct combat jobs, have not been effective at equalizing status opportunities. Of particular note, the committee finds that different physical fitness requirements for male and female soldiers have undermined the status value of those accomplishments for women (see Department of the Army, 2011, for details of the Army Standards of Medical Fitness). Military service members, in speaking with the committee, repeatedly noted the differential respect accorded female soldiers who are held to lower strength and stamina standards. Army soldiers speaking with the committee argued that the Army should determine the necessary physical fitness competency to be an effective solider and then hold all soldiers accountable to that same standard, without adjusting expectations based on gender. Likewise, Deputy chief of staff for operations at the Army's Training and Doctrine Command, David Brinkley, was quoted in the Associated Press (Baldor, 2014): "The men don't want to lower the standards because they see that as a perceived risk to their team . . . The women don't want to lower the standards because they want the men to know they're just as able as they are to do the same task."

As the Army Physical Readiness Training manual recognizes, "the effectiveness of Soldiers depends largely on their physical condition. Full spectrum operations place a premium on the Soldier's strength, stamina, agility, resiliency, and coordination" (Department of the Army, 2012a, p. 1-1). The impact of the current Army policy of unequal standards, rather than increasing status opportunities for women by enabling more of them to qualify for service, has resulted in devaluing the status for women. When asked what a female soldier could do to earn the respect of the elite male soldiers the committee interviewed, one responded, "if she could do ten pull-ups, everyone would respect her." Clearly, differences in physical abilities for men and women are a substantial barrier to status opportunities for women in the military context. Of course, successful soldiers need more than just brawn; but if the social context emphasizes raw physical strength as a gateway to opportunity, it is unclear how women can successfully negotiate status commensurate with the actual value they bring to their units. In the current military context, the achievable status levels of females are limited by organizational policy outside their control; this committee judges this to be a significant issue of human resource management that the Army should care about a great deal.

EFFECTS ON LEADERSHIP CAPABILITIES OF MISALIGNMENT BETWEEN POWER AND STATUS

The discussion so far has focused on status hierarchies that are distinctively important in the modern Army, and especially on opportunities to move up status hierarchies based on status-conferring attributes such as gender. In this section, the committee turns attention to a consequence of status hierarchies that can be a source of problems in the Army: misalignments between power hierarchies (e.g., formal military rank) and status hierarchies (e.g., informal respect and esteem). Misalignments, especially those in which power is greater than status, can produce negative leadership outcomes such as toxic leadership behaviors, which include "dysfunctional behaviors to deceive, intimidate, coerce, or unfairly punish others" (Department of the Army, 2012b, p. 3).

While the criteria for status attainment in the Army are predominantly masculine and related to preparation for combat and combat experience, the criteria for formal rank promotions are broader. Officer promotions, prescribed by 10 U.S.C. § 3001-5000 (2011),[9] are largely based on time-in-grade and performance records (including the officer evaluation report and current and past responsibilities). Promotion methods vary depending on circumstances and need, but an officer "fully qualified" for promotion "is one of demonstrated integrity, who has shown that he or she is qualified professionally and morally to perform the duties expected of an officer in the next higher grade" (Department of the Army, 2005, p. 9.19). Enlisted soldier promotion methods transform over the course of a soldier's career, shifting from strict time-in-grade promotions for junior enlisted soldiers (E-1 to E-4) to NCO local promotion exam boards (E-5 to E-6), in which candidates are scored on a range of items from personal appearance to knowledge of basic soldiering, and then to centralized NCO promotions based on performance records (E-7 to E-9). The potential for misalignment between power and status within a small unit is especially salient when one considers that a platoon is led by its highest ranking member, an officer who is relatively young and inexperienced compared to the years of expe-

[9]See http://www.gpo.gov/fdsys/pkg/CPRT-112HPRT67344/pdf/CPRT-112HPRT67344.pdf [June 2014].

rience of the platoon sergeant. While the Army relies upon effective chain of command protocols and the authority of commanding officers to make decisions that will be followed, disparities in power versus status within a small unit certainly affect collective behaviors and ultimately mission success in ways the Army should seek to better understand.

To be clear, power and status are not entirely independent; they contribute to and influence each other. Rank may act as a status-conferring attribute and status may contribute to a soldier's qualification for promotion in rank. However, to simplify, while the Army's status hierarchy is heavily influenced by status-conferring attributes, such as gender and physical attributes, promotions up the power hierarchy of formal military rank are based on experience, task-relevant skills, and conduct. Because soldiers may advance in power and status hierarchies based on different criteria, a misalignment between power and status may develop, resulting in potentially negative consequences on unit effectiveness and individual careers.

Research on the interactive effects of power and status in other contexts suggests that considering the alignment between these two sources of social influence may help explain a variety of behaviors of interest for the Army. For instance, research on legitimacy implies that aligned power and status are associated with effective leadership (i.e., high power and high status) and deferential followership (i.e., low power and low status) (Tyler, 2006; Ellemers et al., 1993; Johnson et al., 2006; Ridgeway et al., 1994, 1995; Tost, 2011; Berger et al., 1998). However, when leaders have high power and low status, dysfunctional behaviors (e.g., intimidation) may result.

Structurally different opportunities and misaligned social hierarchies may produce dysfunctional behaviors for both the institution and the individuals in it (Fast et al., 2012; Blader and Chen, 2012; Eagly and Karau, 2002; Berdahl, 2007; Rudman et al., 2012; Oldmeadow and Fiske, 2010; Anderson and Brown, 2010). For example, managers who have high power and low status tend to demean subordinates and treat them unjustly (Fast et al., 2012; Blader and Chen, 2012) and so may be more likely to engage in "toxic leadership." For instance, a recent study by Fast and colleagues (2012) determined that leaders with high power and low status are most likely to demean their subordinates by requiring them to do things like bark like a dog or reveal negative traits about themselves. Subordinates are less likely to defer to the authority of high-power superiors whom subordinates don't respect—they have low status (Thomas et al., 1986; Walker et al., 1986; Zelditch and Walker, 1984). Furthermore, the institutional interventions to equalize opportunities to gain power (such as demographically blinded testing procedures) are different from those that may equalize access to status (such as the 2005 creation of the Combat Action Badge to recognize soldiers who engage or are engaged by the enemy, regardless of their branch of service or occupational specialty).[10] In other words, research studies suggest that misaligned power and status (e.g., high power and low status) produce dysfunctional leadership behaviors and less deferential followership.

Dysfunctional behaviors in Army leaders, including self-centered attitudes and motivations, adversely affect subordinates, the organization, and mission performance (Department of the Army, 2012b) and are "associated with low unit cohesion, low subordinate motivation, work quality, and commitment to the Army" (Center for Army Leadership, 2012, p. 3). Yet, dysfunctional leadership behaviors persist in the Army: Recent survey results indicate that 83 percent of soldiers observed a toxic leader in the past year (Center for Army Leadership, 2011) and 1 in 5 soldiers believe their direct supervisor displayed toxic behaviors (Center for Army Leadership, 2012). Before effective policies can be developed to improve this situation, the Army would benefit from a better understanding of the darker sides of leadership (Larsson, 2012) to develop fundamental knowledge of the factors, especially those that may be prevalent in military environments, that influence these behaviors (for a review of recent research on unethical leadership behaviors, see Barling et al., 2010). Research into factors, such as misalignments between power and status in small units, that may influence such behaviors will be important to pursue as the Army moves toward a leaner force where promotions and career service may be more difficult to attain.

The general question of how power and status alignment (or misalignment) impact success in leadership roles and the performance of the units being led by those leaders is of great practical significance in Army contexts. Specifically, how does variance in the respect accorded to higher-ranking soldiers affect their leadership behaviors, from effective to toxic (e.g., engaging in deceit, intimidation, or coercion)? Based on research conducted outside the military, one would expect that the lower the status of higher-ranking soldiers within a small unit, the more likely they are to engage in toxic or less authoritative leadership behaviors. On the other hand, research on transformational leadership in nonmilitary contexts has found that men are more likely to engage in non-optimal leadership behaviors than are women (Eagly et al., 2003), which suggests that it is possible that misalignments between status and power motivate more effective leadership behaviors in some circumstances. Therefore, the committee believes the Army would be well served to investigate how the interaction between

[10]Previously, soldiers outside infantry or Special Forces units did not receive an award for service in combat. Information on U.S. Army awards and decorations is available through the U.S. Army Human Resources Command website, available: https://www.hrc.army.mil/TAGD/Awards%20and%20Decorations%20Branch [April 2014].

power and status may affect leadership capabilities in specifically military contexts, to determine whether and to what extent the research results from civilian contexts apply.

Research on status effects on leadership poses significant challenges requiring innovation in survey and experimental design. It will be methodologically difficult, but not impossible, to tease apart the contributions of a leader's characteristics (individual differences including but not limited to differences that produce status-power discrepancies, i.e., gender, race, sexual orientation, religion), training, characteristics of the troops ("the followers"), and the difficulty of the missions assigned to the unit. In Chapter 4, the committee proposed development of "contextual leadership" (and "followership") assessment tools; such tools should also prove useful in this research on status effects. For example, using newly developed measures of effective leadership and team communication (e.g., assessments of how well the troops understand the commander's intent and the leader's awareness of the overall and individual readiness and motivation levels of his/her troops), research should provide a more refined description of the ramifications of effective and toxic leadership. Furthermore, the new longitudinal survey recommended in Chapter 7 would be useful to establish evidence for causal relationships among factors found to be statistically associated. This could, for instance, begin with surveys of soldiers in Officer Candidate School, with follow-ups throughout their careers, including performance evaluations and surveys of their subordinates' respect and other status-relevant perceptions.

Recognizing the different access opportunities and behavioral implications of attaining positions of power versus status may help explain many behaviors of interest across military environments. In particular, challenges facing nonprototypical soldiers in earning status likely create systematically different opportunities to exercise social influence and informal leadership, such that the Army may be overlooking valuable potential among its troops. For example, Implicit Leadership Theory proposes that people have certain prototypes or idealized visions about what constitutes good leadership for any particular context (Lord and Maher, 1991; Lord et al., 1984). This idealized leader is used as a standard against which actual leaders are compared. If a leader is high on prototypicality it means that he or she is thought to embody the group's norms and values. Although some Implicit Leadership Theory researchers have argued that followers update their mental image of a good unit leader, the empirical data so far do not support this view. Followers' perceptions of who constitutes a good leader appear to be fairly stable over time, despite disconfirming evidence (Epitropaki and Martin, 2005a, 2005b; see also Snyder, 1982; Tinsley et al., 2002). Ultimately, the success of a leader is highly dependent upon whether followers accept the individual as a leader and thereby afford the leader a level of status commensurate with his or her position of power; the importance of followers' perceptions in the leader-follower relationship cannot be overstated.

Furthermore, the inability to gain status may be a factor that contributes to soldiers' engaging in dysfunctional behaviors such as alcoholism, aggression, or suicide, as well as behaviors associated with toxic leadership or other, less extreme, forms of ineffective leadership. Motivation to maintain the status hierarchy may also be related to harassment of low-status unit members who try to negotiate higher status for themselves.

Based on the research summarized above, one would predict that misalignments between power and status may be associated with a range of behaviors of significant importance for small unit effectiveness. In order to study these dynamics effectively, research should be designed with actual Army personnel as the subjects because the particular status values associated with different characteristics and behaviors are specific to the context of Army units. Furthermore, to understand how these ubiquitous social dynamics play out in the Army, research needs to be conducted on them *in situ*.

FUTURE RESEARCH ON DISTINCT SOURCES OF POWER AND STATUS

Conclusion 5
The committee concludes that informal processes of negotiating status (e.g., respect and admiration from peers) are an important source of influence in small units in addition to formal power; these processes have substantial implications for human resource utilization and small unit performance.

Recommendation 5
The U.S. Army Research Institute for the Behavioral and Social Sciences and other U.S. military funding agencies should fund basic research on:

1. **how soldiers gain status;**
2. **how status attainment may differ between men and women and between combat and noncombat functions;**
3. **how the interaction between rank and status may produce positive or negative leadership outcomes; and**
4. **how status affects careers, behavioral outcomes, and small unit effectiveness.**

A RESEARCH METHOD STRATEGY

Many research methods could be employed in the proposed research on negotiated status (e.g., the dynamic processes by which respect and admiration are given by peers) within military environments. An ideal approach would combine experimental and nonexperimental methods, including observational and ethnographic studies. For example, the longitudinal survey recommended in Chapter 7 could be a useful vehicle for nonexperimental studies tracking career paths for soldiers with different ascribed status characteristics and accumulated experiences.

An experimental study could be designed to establish causality by comparing men and women in support versus combat roles in a military training simulation. Small teams could be composed of research participants who all have the same formal ranks in order to hold power equal. They would complete a round-robin questionnaire of each team member's perceptions of every other individual teammate along with self-surveys to assess their expectations of their own and each other teammate's respect, prestige, skills, knowledge, and task competence in the upcoming task.[11] They would then perform the simulated task, and their performance would be captured. Following the task, they would complete another round-robin questionnaire with the same set of questions, followed by questions about the extent to which they felt that (1) they were appropriately respected by other members of the team, (2) they contributed to accomplishing the team's goal, (3) status was important to them in this context, and (4) they were motivated to increase their status in the team. Other questions would ask about any actions, both competitive and collaborative, that they engaged in to increase their status. Videotaped records could also be coded and biosensors or "smart badges" could be used to determine interactive patterns and provide objective process data. In this way, nonintrusive methods based on digital monitoring of interpersonal interactions or periodic qualitative or ethnographic observations could be used to supplement the self-report instruments.

A parallel survey design, sampling respondents from actual units, would provide externally valid answers to questions about how status-enhancing processes in the Army vary by individual differences (e.g., gender) and functional role requirements. The soldiers would be surveyed when first assigned to new units, with a round-robin questionnaire like the one described in the experimental study above. The survey would include ratings of status and competence perceptions and the extent to which they felt respected and influential; it would ask about their motivation to increase

[11]For an example of a round-robin questionnaire format, see http://www.qualtrics.com/qualtrics-360/ [April 2014].

their status and the behaviors in which they have engaged to do so. This survey could be repeated periodically for at least 3 years (assuming the unit membership remains relatively intact during that time so that the same individual unit members complete the survey several times), especially before and after deployments or special training activities.

REFERENCES

Amanatullah, E.T., and C.H. Tinsley. (2013). Punishing female negotiators for asserting too much . . . or not enough: Exploring why advocacy moderates backlash against assertive female negotiators. *Organizational Behavior and Human Decision Processes,* 120(1):110-122.

Anderson, C., and C.E. Brown. (2010). The functions and dysfunctions of hierarchy. *Research in Organizational Behavior,* 30(C):55-89.

Anderson, C., and G.J. Kilduff. (2009). Why do dominant personalities attain influence in face-to-face groups? The competence-signaling effects of trait dominance. *Journal of Personality and Social Psychology,* 96(2):491-503.

Anderson, C., S. Brion, D.A. Moore, and J.A. Kennedy. (2012). A status-enhancement account of overconfidence. *Journal of Personality and Social Psychology,* 103(4):718-735.

Baldor, L.C. (2014). AP Exclusive: Few Army Women Want Combat Jobs. Available: http://bigstory.ap.org/article/ap-exclusive-few-army-women-want-combat-jobs [March 2014].

Bales, R. (1958). Task roles and social roles in problem-solving groups. In E. Maccoby, T. Newcomb, and E. Hartley, Eds., *Readings in Social Psychology,* 3rd ed. (pp. 437-447). New York: Holt, Rinehart, and Winston.

Bales, R.F., F.L. Strodtbeck, T.M. Mills, and M.E. Roseborough. (1951). Channels of communication in small groups. *American Sociological Review,* 16(4):461-468.

Barling, J., A. Christie, and A. Hoption. (2010). Leadership. In S. Zedeck, Ed., *APA Handbook of Industrial and Organizational Psychology* (pp. 183-240). Washington, DC: American Psychological Association.

Beilock, S.L., R.J. Rydell, and A.R. McConnell. (2007). Stereotype threat and working memory: Mechanisms, alleviation, and spill over. *Journal of Experimental Psychology: General,* 136(2):256-276.

Bendersky, C., and N. Shah. (2012). The costs of status enhancement: Performance effects of individual's status mobility in task groups. *Organization Science,* 23(2):308-322.

Berdahl, J.L. (2007). Harassment based on sex: Protecting social status in the context of gender hierarchy. *Academy of Management Review,* 32(2):641-658.

Berger, J. (1977). *Status Characteristics and Social Interaction: An Expectation States Approach.* New York: Elsevier.

Berger, J., B.P. Cohen, and M. Zelditch Jr. (1972). Status characteristics and social interaction. *American Sociological Review,* 37(3):241-255.

Berger, J., T.L. Connor, and M.H. Fisek. (1974). *Expectation States Theory: A Theoretical Research Program.* Cambridge, MA: Winthrop Publishers.

Berger, J., S.J. Rosenholtz, and M. Zelditch Jr. (1980). Status organizing processes. *Annual Review of Sociology,* 6(1):479-508.

Berger, J., M. Webster, C.L. Ridgeway, and S.J. Rosenholtz. (1986). Status cues, expectations, and behavior. In E.J. Lawler, Ed., *Advances in Group Processes,* Vol. 3 (pp. 1-22). Greenwich, CT: JAI Press.

Berger, J., C.L. Ridgeway, M.H. Fisek, and R.Z. Norman. (1998). The legitimation and delegitimation of power and prestige orders. *American Sociological Review,* 63(3):379-405.

Biernat, M., C.S. Crandall, L.V. Young, D. Kobrynowicz, and S.M. Halpin. (1998). All that you can be: Stereotyping of self and others in a military context. *Journal of Personality and Social Psychology,* 75(2):301-317.

Blader, S.L., and Y.R. Chen. (2012). Differentiating the effects of status and power: A justice perspective. *Journal of Personality and Social Psychology,* 102(5):994-1014.

Blau, P. (1970). A formal theory of differentiation in organizations. *American Sociological Review,* 35(2):201-218.

Bunderson, J.S. (2003). Recognizing and utilizing expertise in work groups: A status characteristics perspective. *Administrative Science Quarterly,* 48(4):557-591.

Carli, L.L., and A.H. Eagly. (1999). Gender effects on social influence and emergent leadership. In G.N. Powell, Ed., *Handbook of Gender and Work* (pp. 203-222). Thousand Oaks, CA: Sage.

Center for Army Leadership. (2011). Center for Army Leadership Annual Survey of Army Leadership (CASAL): Army Leader's Perceptions of Army Leaders and Army Leadership Practices. Available: http://usacac.army.mil/CAC2/Repository/CASAL_Participant Feedback_2011_1.pdf [April 2014].

Center for Army Leadership. (2012). 2011 Center for Army Leadership Annual Survey of Army Leadership (CASAL): Main Findings. Leadership Research, Assessment, and Doctrine Division. Fort Leavenworth, KS. Available: http://usacac.army.mil/cac2/repository/CASAL_TechReport2012-1_MainFindings.pdf [April 2014].

Cheng, J.T., J.L. Tracy, T. Foulsham, A. Kingstone, and J. Henrich. (2013). Two ways to the top: Evidence that dominance and prestige are distinct yet viable avenues to social rank and influence. *Journal of Personality and Social Psychology,* 104(1):103-125.

Correll, S., and C. Ridgeway. (2006). Expectation states theory. In J. Delamater, Ed., *Handbook of Social Psychology,* Vol. XVI (pp. 29-51). New York: Springer.

DeKlepper, M., G. Labianca, E. Sleebos, and F. Agneessens. (2013). *The Emergence of the Iron Cage: The Role of Sociometric Status in Establishing a Concertive Control System.* Unpublished paper, Amsterdam University College, the Netherlands.

Department of the Army. (2005). *Officer Promotions. Army Regulation 600-8-29.* Washington, DC: Headquarters, Department of the Army. Available http://www.apd.army.mil/pdffiles/r600_8_29.pdf [February 2014].

Department of the Army. (2008). Unified Land Operations. Army Field Manual 3-0. Washington, DC: Headquarters, Department of the Army. Available: http://downloads.army.mil/fm3-0/FM3-0.pdf [April 2014].

Department of the Army. (2011). *Standards of Medical Fitness. Army Regulation 40-501.* Washington, DC: Headquarters, Department of the Army. Available: http://armypubs.army.mil/epubs/pdf/r40_501.pdf [February 2014].

Department of the Army. (2012a). *Field Manual 7-22, Army Physical Readiness Training.* Washington, DC: Headquarters, Department of the Army. Available: http://armypubs.army.mil/doctrine/DR_pubs/dr_a/pdf/fm7_22.pdf [February 2014].

Department of the Army. (2012b). *Army Doctrine Publication 6-22. Army Leadership.* Washington, DC: Headquarters, Department of the Army. Available: http://armypubs.army.mil/doctrine/DR_pubs/dr_a/pdf/adp6_22_new.pdf [February 2014].

Department of Defense. (2012). *2012 Demographics: Profile of the Military Community.* Office of the Deputy Assistant Secretary of Defense (Military Community and Family Policy). Available: http://www.armyg1.army.mil/hr/docs/demographics/FY12_ARMY_PROFILE.pdf [June 2014].

Department of Defense. (2013). *Department of Defense Annual Report on Sexual Assault in the Military, Fiscal Year 2012.* Volumes 1 and 2. Department of Defense Sexual Assault Prevention and Response. Washington, DC: Department of Defense. Available: http://www.sapr.mil/ [June 2014].

Eagly, A.H., and L.L. Carli. (2003). The female leadership advantage: An evaluation of the evidence. *The Leadership Quarterly,* 14(6):807-834.

Eagly, A.H., and M.C. Johannesen-Schmidt. (2001). The leadership styles of women and men. *Journal of Social Issues,* 57(4):781-797.

Eagly, A.H., and B.T. Johnson. (1990). Gender and leadership-style: A meta-analysis. *Psychology Bulletin,* 108(2):233-256.

Eagly, A.H., and S.J. Karau. (2002). Role congruity theory of prejudice toward female leaders. *Psychological Review,* 109(3):573-598.

Eagly, A.H., S.J. Karau, and M.G. Makhijani. (1995). Gender and the effectiveness of leaders: A meta-analysis. *Psychological Bulletin,* 117(1):125-145.

Eagly, A.H., M.C. Johannesen-Schmidt, and M.L. van Engen. (2003). Transformational, transactional, and laissez-faire leadership styles: A meta-analysis comparing women and men. *Psychological Bulletin,* 129:569-591.

Ellemers, N., H. Wilke, and A. Van Knippenberg. (1993). Effects of the legitimacy of low group or individual status on individual and collective status-enhancement strategies. *Journal of Personality and Social Psychology,* 64(5):766-778.

Emerson, R.M. (1962). Power-dependence relations. *American Sociological Review,* 27(1): 31-41.

Epitropaki, O., and R. Martin. (2005a). From ideal to real: A longitudinal study of implicit leadership theories on leader-member exchanges and employee outcomes. *Journal of Applied Psychology,* 90(4):659-676.

Epitropaki, O., and R. Martin. (2005b). The moderating role of individual differences in the relation between transformational/transactional leadership perceptions and organizational identification. *Leadership Quarterly,* 16(4):569-589.

Faris, R. (2012). Aggression, exclusivity, and status attainment in interpersonal networks. *Social Forces,* 90(4):1,207-1,235.

Faris, R., and D. Felmlee. (2011). Status struggles: Network centrality and gender segregation in same- and cross-gender aggression. *American Sociological Review,* 76(1):48-73.

Fast, N.J., N. Halevy, and A.D. Galinsky. (2012). The destructive nature of power without status. *Journal of Experimental Social Psychology,* 48(1):391-394.

Fiske, S.T., A.J.C. Cuddy, P. Glick, and J. Xu. (2002). A model of (often mixed) stereotype content: Competence and warmth respectively follow from perceived status and competition. *Journal of Personality and Social Psychology,* 82(6):878-902.

Fiske, S.T., A.J.C. Cuddy, and P. Glick. (2007). Universal dimensions of social cognition: Warmth and competence. *Trends in Cognitive Science,* 11(2):77-83.

Flynn, F.J., R.E. Reagans, E.T. Amanatullah, and D.R. Ames. (2006). Helping one's way to the top: Self-monitors achieve status by helping others and knowing who helps whom. *Journal of Personality and Social Psychology,* 91(6):1,123-1,137.

Fragale, A.R. (2006). The power of powerless speech: The effects of speech style and task interdependence on status conferral. *Organizational Behavior and Human Decision Processes,* 101(2):243-261.

Fragale, A.R., J.R. Overbeck, and M.A. Neale. (2011). Resources versus respect: Social judgments based on targets' power and status positions. *Journal of Experimental Social Psychology,* 47(4):767-775.

French, J.R.P., and B. Raven. (1959). The bases of social power. In D. Cartwright, Ed., *Studies in Social Power* (pp. 150-167). Ann Arbor, MI: University of Michigan Press.

Goffman, E. (1967). *Interaction Ritual: Essays on Face-to-Face Behavior.* Chicago, IL: Aldine.

Goldhamer, H., and E.A. Shils. (1939). Types of power and status. *American Journal of Sociology,* 45(2):171-182.

Gould, R.V. (2003). *Collision of Wills: How Ambiguity about Social Rank Breeds Conflict.* Chicago, IL: University of Chicago Press.

Hardy, C.L., and M. Van Vugt. (2006). Nice guys finish first: The competitive altruism hypothesis. *Personality and Social Psychology Bulletin,* 32(10):1,402-1,413.

Harrell, M.C., L. Werber Castaneda, P. Schirmer, B.W. Hallmark, J. Kavanagh, D. Gershwin, P. Steinberg. (2007). *Assessing the Assignment Policy for Army Women.* Santa Monica, CA: RAND National Defense Research Institute. Available: http://www.rand.org/content/dam/rand/pubs/monographs/2007/RAND_MG590-1.pdf [May 2014].

Heilman, M.E. (2012). Gender stereotypes and workplace bias. *Research in Organizational Behavior,* 32:113-135.

Heilman, M.E., and T.G. Okimoto. (2007). Why are women penalized for success at male tasks?: The implied communality deficit. *Journal of Applied Psychology,* 92(1):81-92.

Heilman, M.E., A.S. Wallen, D. Fuchs, and M.M. Tamkins. (2004). Penalties for success: Reactions to women who succeed at male gender-typed tasks. *Journal of Applied Psychology,* 89(3):416-427.

Hofstede, G.H. (1980). *Culture's Consequences: International Differences in Work-Related Values.* Beverly Hills, CA: Sage Publications.

Huberman, B.A., C.H. Loch, and A. Önçüler. (2004). Status as a valued resource. *Social Psychology Quarterly,* 67(1):103-114.

Ickes, W.J., and E.S. Knowles. (1982). *Personality, Roles, and Social Behavior.* New York: Springer-Verlag.

International Security Assistance Force. (2011). *Engaging the Female Populace.* Kabul, Afghanistan: International Security Assistance Force. Available: http://info.publicintelligence.net/ISAF-FemaleEngagement.pdf [June 2014].

Johnson, C., T.J. Dowd, and C.L. Ridgeway. (2006). Legitimacy as a social process. *Annual Review of Sociology,* 32(1):53-78.

Jost, J.T., B.W. Pelham, and M.R. Carvallo. (2002). Non-conscious forms of system justification: Implicit and behavioral preferences for higher status groups. *Journal of Experimental Social Psychology,* 38(6):586-602.

Kanter, R. M. (1977). *Men and Women of the Corporation.* New York: Basic Books.

Keltner, D., D.H. Gruenfeld, and C. Anderson. (2003). Power, approach, and inhibition. *Psychological Review,* 110(2):265-284.

Kray, L.J., and L. Thompson. (2005). Gender stereotypes and negotiation performance: An examination of theory and research. *Research in Organizational Behavior,* 26:103-182.

Kray, L.J., L. Thompson, and A. Galinsky. (2001). Battle of the sexes: Gender stereotype confirmation and reactance in negotiations. *Journal of Personality and Social Psychology,* 80(6):942-958.

Larsson, G. (2012). Leader development in a natural context. In J.H. Laurence and M.D. Matthews, Eds., *The Oxford Handbook of Military Psychology* (pp. 187-196). New York: Oxford University Press.

Lord, R.G., and K.J. Maher. (1991). *Leadership and Information Processing: Linking Perceptions and Organizational Performance.* Boston, MA: Rutledge.

Lord, R.G., R.J. Foti, and C.L. De Vader. (1984). A test of leadership categorization theory: Internal structure, information processing, and leadership perceptions. *Organizational Behavior and Human Performance,* 34(3):343-378.

Lucas, J.W. (2003). Status processes and the institutionalization of women as leaders. *American Sociological Review,* 68(3):464-480.

Magee, J.C., and A.D. Galinsky. (2008). Social hierarchy: The self-reinforcing nature of power and status. *The Academy of Management Annals,* 2(1):351-398.

Mazur, A. (1973). A cross-species comparison of status in small established groups. *American Sociological Review,* 38(5):513-530.

National Women's Law Center. (2013). *Restrictions on Assignments of Military Women: A Brief History.* Washington, DC: National Women's Law Center. Available: http://www.nwlc.org/sites/default/files/pdfs/women_in_military_assignments_a_brief_history_revised_may_2013.pdf [June 2014].

Oldmeadow, J.A., and S.T. Fiske. (2010). Social status and the pursuit of positive social identity: Systematic domains of intergroup differentiation and discrimination for high- and low-status groups. *Group Processes and Intergroup Relations,* 13(4):425-444.

Pettit, N.C., K. Yong, and S.E. Spataro. (2010). Holding your place: Reactions to the prospect of status gains and losses. *Journal of Experimental Social Psychology,* 46(2):396-401.

Podolny, J.M. (2005). *Status Signals: A Sociological Study of Market Competition.* Princeton, NJ: Princeton University Press.

Podolny, J.M., and J.N. Baron. (1997). Resources and relationships: Social networks and mobility in the workplace. *American Sociological Review,* 62(5):673-693.

Pronin, E., C.M. Steele, and L. Ross. (2004). Identity bifurcation in response to stereotype threat: Women and mathematics. *Journal of Experimental Social Psychology,* 40(2): 152-168.

Ridgeway, C.L. (1982). Status in groups: The importance of motivation. *American Sociological Review,* 47(1):76-87.

Ridgeway, C.L. (1987). Nonverbal behavior, dominance, and the basis of status in task groups. *American Sociological Review,* 52(5):683-694.

Ridgeway, C.L. (1991). The social construction of status value: Gender and other nominal characteristics. *Social Forces,* 70(2):367-386.

Ridgeway, C.L., and J.W. Balkwell. (1997). Group processes and the diffusion of status beliefs. *Social Psychology Quarterly,* 60(1):14-31.

Ridgeway, C.L., and J. Berger. (1986). Expectations, legitimation, and dominance behavior in task groups. *American Sociological Review,* 51(5):603-617.

Ridgeway, C.L., and D. Diekema. (1989). Dominance and collective hierarchy formation in male and female task groups. *American Sociological Review,* 54(1):79-93.

Ridgeway, C.L., and K.G. Erickson. (2000). Creating and spreading status beliefs. *American Journal of Sociology,* 106(3):579-615.

Ridgeway, C.L., C. Johnson, and D. Diekema. (1994). External status, legitimacy, and compliance in male and female groups. *Social Forces,* 72(4):1,051-1,077.

Ridgeway, C.L., D. Diekema, and C. Johnson. (1995). Legitimacy, compliance, and gender in peer groups. *Social Psychology Quarterly,* 58(4):298-311.

Ridgeway, C.L., E.H. Boyle, K.J. Kuipers, and D.T. Robinson. (1998). How do status beliefs develop? The role of resources and interactional experience. *American Sociological Review,* 63(3):331-350.

Rudman, L.A., and S.E. Kilianski. (2000). Implicit and explicit attitudes towards female authority. *Personality and Social Psychology Bulletin,* 26(11):1,315-1,328.

Rudman, L.A., C.A. Moss-Racusin, J.E. Phelan, and S. Nauts. (2012). Status incongruity and backlash effects: Defending the gender hierarchy motivates prejudice against female leaders. *Journal of Experimental Social Psychology,* 48(1):165-179.

Russell, B. (1938). *Power: A New Social Analysis.* New York: W.W. Norton and Co.

Sampson, E.E. (1963). Status congruence and cognitive consistency. *Sociometry,* 26(2):146-162.

Schwartz, S. (1994). Beyond individualism/collectivism: new dimensions of values. In U. Kim, H. Triandis, C. Kagitcibasi, S. Choi, and G. Yoon, Eds., *Individualsm and Collectivism: Theory, Application and Methods* (pp. 85-122). Thousand Oaks, CA: Sage.

Sidanius, J., and F. Pratto. (1993). The inevitability of oppression and the dynamics of social dominance. In P.M. Sniderman, P.E. Tetlock, and E. Carmies, Eds., *Prejudice, Politics, and the American Dilemma* (pp. 173-211). Stanford, CA: Stanford University Press.

Snyder, M. (1982). Self-fulfilling stereotypes. *Psychology Today,* July:60-88.

Steele, C.M., and J. Aronson. (1995). Stereotype threat and the intellectual test performance of African Americans. *Journal of Personality and Social Psychology,* 69(5):797-811.

Strauss, A.L. (1978). *Negotiations: Varieties, Contexts, Processes, and Social Order.* San Francisco, CA: Jossey-Bass.

Strauss, A.L., L. Schatzman, R. Bucher, D. Ehrlich, and M. Sabshin. (1963). The hospital and its negotiated order. In E. Friedson, Ed., *Hospital in Modern Society* (pp. 147-169). New York: Free Press.

Thomas, G.M., H.A. Walker, and M. Zelditch Jr. (1986). Legitimacy and collective action. *Social Forces,* 65(2):378-404.

Tiedens, L.Z., M.M. Unzueta, and M.J. Young. (2007). An unconscious desire for hierarchy? The motivated perception of dominance complementarity in task partners. *Journal of Personality and Social Psychology,* 93(3):402-414.

Tinsley, C.H., K. O'Connor, and B. Sullivan. (2002). "Tough" guys finish last: The perils of a distributive reputation. *Organization Behavior and Human Decision Processes,* 88:621-642.

Tost, L.P. (2011). An integrative model of legitimacy judgments. *Academy of Management Review,* 36(4):686-710.

Tyler, T.R. (2006). Psychological perspectives on legitimacy and legitimation. *Annual Review of Psychology,* 57:375-400.

Walker, H.A., G.M. Thomas, and M. Zelditch Jr. (1986). Legitimation, endorsement, and stability. *Social Forces,* 64(3):620-643.

Willer, R. (2009). Groups reward individual sacrifice: The status solution to the collective action problem. *American Sociological Review,* 74(1):23-43.

Williams, K.Y., and C.A. O'Reilly. (1998). Demography and diversity in organizations: A review of 40 years of research. *Research in Organizational Behavior,* 20:77-140.

Zelditch, M. Jr., and H.A. Walker. (1984). Legitimacy and the stability of authority. In E.E. Lawler, Ed., *Advances in Group Processes,* Vol. 1 (pp. 1-27). Greenwich, CT: JAI Press.

6

Multiteam Systems as the Context for Individuals and Teams

The Army has long been structured around teams as the basic unit of work.[1] Teams enable individuals to accomplish two critical aspects of military work: work "at scale" and work that is highly complex. The Army is a full-scale organization, which must accomplish varied missions ranging from special operations and provincial reconstruction to stability and support. First, teams enable individuals to scale up effort in order to accomplish enormous tasks by pooling their effort. Second, teams enable military work by facilitating the specialization of labor. Individuals can be selected for particular jobs, trained for those jobs, and develop deep expertise. By working in teams, individuals transcend the limitations of their narrow but deep knowledge and skill sets. However, as the complexity of military operations has increased, the basic unit of work accomplishment in the Army, and across the military services, is shifting from teams to teams-of-teams, often called multiteam systems (MTSs). Accordingly, the teams and MTSs that soldiers work in every day are influential aspects of their context (DeChurch and Zaccaro, 2010).

For the purposes of this report, the committee adopts the following definition of an MTS (Mathieu et al., 2001, p. 290):

> Two or more teams that interface directly and interdependently in response to environmental contingencies toward the accomplishment of collective goals. MTS boundaries are defined by virtue of the fact that all teams

[1]Within this chapter of the report only, the term "team" is applied generally to refer to groups of people working together to accomplish a goal. This includes, but is not limited to, Army small units.

> within the system, while pursuing different proximal goals, share at least one common distal goal; and in doing so exhibit input, process and outcome interdependence with at least one other team in the system.

Mathieu and colleagues (2001) apply the MTS concept to understand the nature of interdependence among the teams that respond to the scene of an automobile accident. Teams drawn from different organizations—emergency medical technicians, firefighters, police, surgeons, and recovery units—all work toward specialized team goals (e.g., the firefighters extract the victim from the automobile), while at the same time working across teams to accomplish a shared MTS goal (e.g., all teams responding to the accident seek to save lives).

In military environments, a similar interdependence exists among small units with distinct equipment, training, and objectives that work with other small units to achieve a single mission. Specifically, research into MTSs may help the Army answer questions such as:

- How do trust and cohesion (affective properties) develop within MTSs? What conditions foster the emergence of desirable affective properties and mitigate the emergence of undesirable ones?
- How do shared mental models and transactive memory systems (cognitive properties that describe knowledge held in common or distributed among team members) develop within MTSs?
- How do MTS members develop confidence in the collective and willingness to put forth effort for the good of the group (motivational properties)?
- What conditions (i.e., compositional, linkage, and developmental attributes of MTSs) foster desirable properties and mitigate the emergence of undesirable ones?
- What are the positive and negative consequences of affective, cognitive, and motivational properties of the MTS for individual readiness, team readiness, and MTS functioning?
- What situational factors (e.g., deployed context) moderate the effects of MTS properties on outcomes (i.e., individual, team, and system)?
- If undesirable properties develop, how can "early warning" detection systems be implemented for leadership to use to reshape these properties?
- What interventions/countermeasures can be used to regulate the development of properties in teams, between teams, and in systems of teams?

There are three defining features of MTSs (Zaccaro et al., 2012):

1. They are minimally composed of at least two component teams.
2. Individuals within MTSs work toward hierarchically arranged goals; goals at the lower level require coordination with the members of their component team, whereas higher level goals require greater coordination with other teams.
3. Interactions between teams in the MTS are driven by various degrees of task interdependencies among component teams.

The MTS resides at a unit of analysis higher than the team, but smaller than the organization. MTSs are "teams of teams." MTSs can be composed of teams from within a single organization, such as the Army, or can include teams drawn from multiple organizations. Goodwin and colleagues (2012) offer rich descriptions MTSs that involve Army units. These MTSs can consist of small units and teams within the Army, or they can involve Army teams with teams from other organizations. For example, the traditional military headquarters is an MTS consisting of a command team overseeing small units that focus on different goals. One staff section pursues personnel goals, another intelligence goals, another pursues operations and logistics goals, and so forth. Each of these staff sections works as a team to achieve its unique goals, while also working with the other staff sections to pursue the broader goals of the headquarters. The decisions of one staff section, for instance the personnel group, set constraints on and require resources from other groups, in this case operations and logistics.

Army teams can be embedded in "all Army" multiteam systems, such as the one just described, but they can also be embedded in cross-organizational MTSs. Goodwin and colleagues (2012) provide a vivid example of the challenges of these collaborations involving military and nonmilitary units drawn from organizations that can have very different, even conflicting goals, as well as different cultures and motivational states. Task Force Phoenix was an MTS with the goal to improve the security of the local people. The teams that worked interdependently toward this goal were drawn from the U.S. military, the U.S./Allied military (which includes soldiers from NATO partner nations), the host nation's police forces, and the host nation's military. Although these teams had to work closely to achieve the MTS's security goal, the teams' embeddedness in four different organizational/national contexts created additional pressures that tended to pull the teams apart. For example, as the authors describe, in Task Force Phoenix law enforcement officers and military soldiers represented organizational cultures with different assumptions about "bad guys." Law enforcement officers hold a fundamental perspective that "bad guys are to be arrested and brought to justice under the law." In contrast, military soldiers hold the perspective that, "bad guys are to be defeated . . . so as to remove their ability to fight" (Goodwin et al., 2012, p. 70).

When MTS component teams are drawn from different embedding organizations, as in the example of Task Force Phoenix, there can be many potential sources of friction (including differences in technological reliance for coordination) and differences in structure (e.g., organization into hierarchies with strong versus weak chains of command). Of particular significance, even when teams are embedded within a single organization, differences between teams' level of experience, functional specialization, etc., can exert no less powerful forces pulling the teams apart and harming the capacity for the MTS to function as a coherent system.

Teams can also be a part of multiple MTSs at any given time, working with different component teams in each. Hence, the traditional Army small units (e.g., squads and platoons) can be, but are not necessarily, MTSs. MTS collectives often connect military units to groups working in other organizations, to accomplish tasks that require coordination across agencies (e.g., joint forces) and nations (e.g., international task forces), as well as spanning the military-civilian divide (e.g., provincial reconstruction teams).

Teams have long been recognized as providing a valuable entity for understanding the most salient aspects of an individual's immediate work context (Edmondson, 1999; Kozlowski and Ilgen, 2006). When work becomes the province of specialized teams, a second set of integration challenges arises as these teams work together as complex systems. From a military MTS perspective, the individual soldier is affected not only by the context of that soldier's immediate small unit but also by other teams, both military and civilian, U.S. and foreign, with whom that soldier's unit interacts (Goodwin et al., 2012).

This chapter unfolds in two parts. First, the committee details the essential elements of the MTS as an organizational form and summarizes current evidence as it relates to the committee's charge to understand the context of military environments. Second, we describe a potential research strategy to advance fundamental understanding of the context of military behavior from the MTS perspective, which culminates in the committee's recommendation for basic research on MTSs as one element of the proposed research agenda.

THE MULTITEAM SYSTEM AS AN ORGANIZATIONAL FORM

The MTS was identified as an organizational form 13 years ago (Mathieu et al., 2001). Findings are beginning to accumulate with important insights into the elements of social context that affect not only individual behavior but the behavior of small teams as well. In fact, just as teams are the immediate context for individual behavior, MTSs are the most proximate context for team behavior. As an example, if a small unit in the Army (in-group) is working closely with another unit (out-group) that the in-group members perceive to be very different from their own unit (e.g., a host nation police force), this will strengthen the internal cohesion of the (in-group) Army unit (Hogg and Terry, 2000). This is an example of how interaction with other teams as a part of larger systems can constitute an important aspect of a unit's social context.

One of the most valuable aspects of the MTS perspective is that it enables context to be understood as arising from entities that are not located within the same embedded organization. Because the scope of many military operations puts small units in direct contact with foreign and nonmilitary units, these entities serve as an important part of the context of military environments. MTSs are not defined by formal organizational hierarchies (i.e., as represented by a standard organizational chart). A unit's context includes those interdependent entities with whom the focal team works. If one were to try to understand a unit's context by only looking at formal structures, an important source of context would be missed. MTSs are defined by actual workflows—through identification of the individuals and teams that need to work together in order to accomplish a mission. The remainder of this section summarizes the literature on MTSs as they relate to individual and team context in military settings (DeChurch and Mathieu, 2009; Marks et al., 2005; Mathieu et al., 2001; Zaccaro et al., 2012).

MTS Composition, Linkage, and Development

The effectiveness of an MTS can be explained through a generic systems model with three sets of MTS attributes (i.e., how the MTS is composed and organized) that serve as inputs into MTS processes (i.e., characteristics of how the MTS functions) (Zaccaro et al., 2012). The three types of MTS attributes are compositional attributes, linkage attributes, and developmental attributes. When teams work as part of an MTS, the compositional, linkage, and developmental attributes of that MTS are valuable for diagnosing the salient aspects of the context of the team. For example, the compositional attribute of diversity can have varying effects on cohesion, a group property that characterizes how strongly members internalize the core values of the team and work toward shared goals. Within an MTS, the diversity of each of the teams, as well as the diversity of the set of teams in the system, plays a role in shaping how the cohesive properties of the teams evolve. Teams low in diversity tend to be more internally cohesive than those with high diversity. When teams work with very different teams, their internal cohesion increases but the cohesion of the larger system tends to decrease.

Compositional Attributes

Compositional attributes refer to "the overall demographic features of the MTS, as well as the relative characteristics of component teams" (Zaccaro et al., 2012, p. 13). They include qualities such as the size of the MTS, the number of its individual team members, where the teams come from, and their diversity on several dimensions. One important compositional attribute is the degree to which MTS component teams are drawn from one larger organization (sometimes called "embedded MTSs") or from different organizations (cross-boundary MTSs).

In a cross-boundary MTS, the component teams that must work together are themselves embedded in different organizations (e.g., the teams described in the auto accident scenario by Mathieu et al., 2001). The challenges of between-team coordination among teams in the MTS may be complicated by differences in organizational culture, operating procedures, or other constraints that affect some teams but not others. Cross-boundary MTSs abound in deployed military operations where teams from the U.S. military must work closely with international and nongovernmental organizations (Goodwin et al., 2012). Given the challenges that arise in cross-boundary MTSs and the lack of empirical research on them, the committee believes that studying them should be a priority in future Army research on social and organizational factors.

Linkage Attributes

Linkage attributes refer to the "linking mechanisms that connect component teams" (Zaccaro et al., 2012, p. 18) and include such features as the degree of interdependence among component teams, the leadership and power arrangements among such teams, and communication structures within the MTS. Of the three sets of MTS attributes, linkage attributes have received the most research attention. In fact, the research on MTS linkage attributes has been largely fueled by military research agencies, perhaps because it aligns well within existing programs on team decision making, organizational effectiveness, and leadership within, for example, the U.S. Air Force Office of Scientific Research and the U.S. Army Research Institute for the Behavioral and Social Sciences (ARI). Studies on linkage attributes have thus far focused on leadership (e.g., DeChurch and Marks, 2006; DeChurch et al., 2011), coordination (e.g., Davison et al., 2012; Marks et al., 2005), and planning (e.g., Lanaj et al., 2013).

Empirical studies of MTS leadership have found that leadership functions (e.g., planning, coordination) need to be shifted from focusing solely on processes within a component team to focusing on integrating component teams. Effective MTS leaders use functional leadership behaviors such as planning and coordination, but focus them on the interactions of a team across its boundaries with other teams, rather than inside its boundary, thereby integrating the efforts of the small team into the larger system. They use planning efforts as a way to *contextualize* what the team is doing in terms of the efforts of other teams (DeChurch and Marks, 2006). These positive between-team leadership behaviors have been linked to what is formally known as *between-team process* (Marks et al., 2005). Based on its review of the research on MTS leadership, the committee finds that leadership behaviors with this shift in focus are an effective way to foster between-team processes.

Other research on MTS leadership suggests that these between-team processes need to be enacted by formal leader teams, not by the teams themselves (Davison et al., 2012). Boundary-spanning attempts by the teams themselves were detrimental to MTS performance for two reasons. First, decentralized planning led to coordination failures. Having more individuals in the MTS engaged in planning increased the chances that teams would act discordantly. The complexity of managing a system of teams requires that a subset of boundary spanners do the planning, while system components refrain from improvisation. This challenge of coordination failures is well understood by Army leaders who seek unity in command and centralized planning that allows for decentralized execution though mission command. A second reason why decentralized planning was harmful to MTS performance was that it increased risk-seeking behavior. Having more individuals in the MTS engaged in planning diffused responsibility (Whyte, 1993). This set of findings is particularly useful to understanding MTSs operating in deployed settings where U.S. military leadership must connect its units to those of other organizations. In essence, these settings make it difficult to establish a purely centralized command structure that would serve to integrate the different teams drawn from the U.S. military with coalition partners or a host nation's military.

Based on the importance of leadership to military operations, and the initial findings that certain patterns of leadership are better than others for facilitating between-team processes, the committee believes that further research should be conducted that explicitly explores the effect of leadership arrangements on between-team processes. The preceding chapter on status hierarchies summarizes an important body of research suggesting that, when people work in groups, they show a need to differentiate status and to develop a shared understanding within the group of who has higher status and who has less. Hence, the status hierarchy perspective is a promising way to investigate leadership "between-teams."

A second set of studies on MTS linkage attributes examines coordination processes in MTSs. These studies distinguish within-team coordination from between-team coordination. *Within-team coordination* is defined as individuals' timing and sequencing of interdependent actions through verbal or behavioral means (Marks et al., 2001). *Between-team coordination* is the timing, sequencing, and integration of team actions with those of other teams (Marks et al., 2005). A repeated observation in conceptual and empirical research on MTSs is that between-team coordination is more difficult to achieve than within-team coordination (Davison et al., 2012; DeChurch and Zaccaro, 2010). A second finding is that between-team coordination is more important to MTS performance than is within-team coordination (Davison et al., 2012; DeChurch and Marks, 2006; Marks et al., 2005). Based on its review of the research, the committee finds that between-team processes are more predictive of MTS performance than are within-team processes.

One consequence of these findings is that the military is seeking to develop ways to facilitate between-team processes.[2] Often these between-team processes are intended to enable military teams to work effectively with nonmilitary and/or international entities. This creates conditions where the processes and properties of military teams are affected by interactions occurring outside the team. Furthermore, there is a very real possibility that there are both positive and negative effects of between-team interaction. This prospect is perhaps most salient when military MTSs require close coordination among U.S. military teams and teams from the civilian sector and/or foreign militaries. In these situations, the coordination required may in fact weaken the normal effectiveness of the military leadership structure and other mechanisms through which unity of command and commander's intent have traditionally been maintained. Thus, the committee believes the Army would benefit from basic research to examine the consequences of MTS support systems on (a) individual performance, (b) team outcomes, and (c) leadership effectiveness.

A recent study on MTS planning provides initial evidence that some between-team processes are both beneficial and harmful to MTS performance (Lanaj et al., 2013). Between-team planning was found to benefit MTS performance by way of increased motivation. Decentralized planning among component teams increased individuals' proactivity and aspiration levels, both of which benefit MTS performance. However, decentralized planning also increased the teams' affinity for risk, which ultimately harmed MTS performance.

---

[2]For example, see Broad Agency Announcement (BAA) W911NF-13-R-0001 (2013). Available: https://www.fbo.gov/?s=opportunity&mode=form&id=102faad5082fa9d2881ec483fe166c2b&tab=core&_cview=1 [June 2014].

Developmental Attributes

The last set of MTS attributes pertains to the "developmental dynamics and patterns" (Zaccaro et al., 2012, p. 20) that characterize the formation and growth of the MTS. These attributes include such factors as whether the MTS is appointed or self-organizes from multiteam interactions, the expected duration of the MTS, and the fluidity of membership within MTS component teams and across the set of teams that comprise the MTS (i.e., the frequency of personnel changes within any particular team that is part of the MTS, and the frequency of instances in which a component team is reassigned to another mission and replaced with a different team).

MTS development has received little attention in the literature, likely due to the logistical challenges of doing controlled research on large, complex systems over time. However, the committee believes this is an important area in need of research attention. Research on MTS development is particularly important to inform military policies on deployment, rotation, and MTS staffing. For example, research is needed to uncover the effects on between-team processes and properties of membership churn within MTS component teams versus teams that remain intact. Given the practical importance of understanding development for military staffing practices, the committee suggests that the study of MTS development, particularly examination of team rotation and fluidity within MTSs, be a priority in future research. For this research to have a real impact, it will need to be conducted with a multiyear commitment to collect longitudinal data (see Chapter 7) capable of capturing details of MTSs as they evolve over time through iterations of the Army Force Generation's 3-year cycle (Department of the Army, 2011).

MTS Processes

These three sets of MTS attributes—compositional, linkage, and developmental—were proposed by Zaccaro and colleagues (2012) to influence MTS outcomes through their effects on MTS interaction processes and properties. MTS success rests on effective processes and interactions occurring both within and among component teams (Marks et al., 2005). Marks and colleagues (2001) delineated several processes that can occur within teams as they accomplish tasks. These included transition, action, and interpersonal processes. *Transition processes* typically occur within planning phases of team performance episodes and include such activities as mission analysis, goal specification, strategy formulation, and action planning. *Action processes* typically occur during execution phases of team performance episodes and include progress monitoring, systems monitoring, team backup behavior, and coordination. *Interpersonal processes* can occur within and outside team performance episodes and include activities such as conflict management, fostering of team motivation, and regulation of team member affect.

Several MTS researchers have extended this process framework to describe the interaction processes that connect component teams within MTSs (i.e., between-team processes). Between-team processes were briefly considered earlier in the discussion of linkage attributes. These studies (Davison et al., 2012; Lanaj et al., 2013) highlight the necessity of examining MTS effectiveness in terms of multilevel processes.

Team and Multiteam Properties

A second set of intervening mechanisms through which MTS attributes relate to individual, team, and system outcomes are MTS properties. Research on small teams supports the distinction between team processes and properties (Cronin et al., 2011; Marks et al., 2001). Team properties, examples of which are cohesion, trust, and efficacy, characterize how strong or weak the team is as a social force that regulates the thoughts and behaviors of its members. Formally defined, *team properties* (which have also been called *emergent states* in the literature on teams) refer to characteristics of the team "that are typically dynamic in nature and vary as a function of team context, inputs, processes, and outcomes" (Marks et al., 2001, p. 357). In a team with strong properties, members' behavior will be shaped and constrained by the team's norms and values to a much greater degree than in a team with weak properties. Research on team properties finds that properties are highly diagnostic in understanding and predicting the future behavior of team members. In fact, team properties are more stable than are interaction processes, and they are more predictive of team outcomes than are team processes (DeChurch et al., 2013). Team processes are directly observable through team interaction and provide a valuable way to change team properties. Over the course of team development, processes regularize into team properties (Gersick and Hackman, 1990), which in turn shape and constrain subsequent behavioral processes. Team properties evolve through team interactions as members interact with one another over time (Curseu, 2006; Kozlowski and Chao, 2012; Klein and Kozlowski, 2000). This duality of structure and process was elaborated by early systems theorists as "reciprocal forces such that interaction processes stabilize over time and emerge to form structures that then shape subsequent processes" (Kozlowski and Chao, 2012, p. 336). Marks and colleagues (2001; see also DeChurch and Mesmer-Magnus, 2010) defined several categories of team properties, including affective, cognitive, and motivational properties. These three categories map onto the basic human functions of "thinking" and "feeling." Cognitive properties are thought patterns in teams that arise from individual's beliefs and expectations. Affective and motivational properties are patterns that grow out of individuals' emotions.

More specifically, the affective properties are properties of a collective that come about through a combination of individuals' emotions. Two examples of affective properties are team trust (Costa, 2003; DeJong and Elfring, 2010) and team cohesion (Festinger, 1950; Mullen and Copper, 1994). Cognitive properties describe the manner in which knowledge that is important to team functioning is mentally organized, represented, and distributed within the team to allow team members to anticipate one another's needs (e.g., who needs to know what, when) and coordinate their work (DeChurch and Mesmer-Magnus, 2010). Some cognitive properties describe the knowledge that must be held in common or understood similarly by all team members; such knowledge is also referred to as "shared mental models" (Mathieu et al., 2000). Other cognitive properties describe knowledge that should be distributed among members to increase the attentional and memory capacity of the team; such knowledge is also referred to as "transactive memory systems" (Ellis, 2006; Lewis, 2003; Zhang et al., 2007). Shared mental models are cognitive schema understood similarly by all team members. Transactive memory systems reflect a division of labor where each member becomes the expert on a particular subset of knowledge, freeing other members to specialize in other knowledge sets. Teams with highly differentiated transactive memory systems can retain more information and can use this information to the extent that members have an accurate understanding of who knows what.

Motivational properties characterize members' confidence in the collective and their willingness to put forth effort for the good of the group. Two widely studied motivational properties are collective efficacy and goal states (Gully et al., 2002).

In MTSs, team properties come about at multiple levels. Whereas team properties are patterns of individuals' thoughts, beliefs, and feelings about the team, *between-team properties* are a team's collective thoughts, beliefs, and feelings about the other teams in the MTS and *MTS properties* characterize a team's thoughts, beliefs, and feelings about the MTS as a whole. Team properties are valuable for understanding how strong or weak the team is as a force that shapes the behavior of its members. In the same way, MTS properties are valuable for understanding how strong or weak an MTS is as a force that shapes the behavior of its component teams.

Recent studies have begun to examine between-team and MTS properties. Jimenez-Rodriguez (2012) measured between-team efficacy by asking team members to indicate how confident they were that their team and another team could achieve its goals. She also asked members to evaluate the perceived competence of the MTS as a whole in achieving its goals (i.e., MTS efficacy). Jimenez-Rodriguez (2012) assessed between-team trust by examining each team's perceptions of "willingness . . . to be vulnerable to the actions of [the other] party" (Mayer et al., 1995, p. 712). She also included in her study measures of shared mental models and transactive memory systems, using the MTS as the referent. Thus, in her study she examined the affective and motivational states that can emerge between two component teams in an MTS, as well as the motivational and cognitive states that can emerge at the system level.

DiRosa (2013) provides additional insight into the nature of MTS cohesion. In a study of Army platoons, DiRosa found complex relationships between the development of small unit cohesion, e.g., how cohesive a squad feels as a small unit, and the development of between-team cohesion, i.e., how cohesive a set of squads feels about one another as a unit. An insight from her field data collection reveals that the extent to which squad and between-squad cohesion are related to each other depends on the level of squad cohesion. The relationship followed an inverted-S such that when squads are very low or very high on cohesion, there is also strong positive relation between squad and "between-squad" cohesion. Stated differently, feeling attached to the squad benefits attachment to the larger collective. However, at moderate levels of squad cohesion, there is no relationship between squad and "between-squad" cohesion. In moderately cohesive squads, the squad may or may not cohere to the larger system.

Taken together, this work indicates that just as combinations of within- and between-team processes have critical implications for overall MTS effectiveness, so do within-team, between-team, and MTS properties. As stated above, properties are more stable characteristics of MTSs than are processes. Processes, which are routinized behavioral patterns shaped by repeated interaction, are inherently more dynamic than properties (DeChurch et al., 2013). Between-team and MTS properties constitute meaningful dimensions of the social context of an MTS. These properties shape and constrain the behavior of individuals and teams. In this way they have predictive value for understanding subsequent behavior across a variety of situations. Team and MTS properties can be thought of as norms that develop within teams, between teams, and in MTSs (see Chapter 2).

MTS properties suggest one valuable way to leverage research on MTSs toward understanding social and organizational factors in the context of military environments. They provide an important conceptual grounding for understanding the nature and strength of these factors within the teams and also between different teams working as a system. In the committee's assessment, research on teams indicates that understanding collective attitudes and beliefs is likely to enable the prediction of a wide range of subsequent behavior in teams. Therefore, future research on MTSs should explore the relationship between MTS properties and behavior within

MTSs. We now turn attention to an exemplar research program designed to enhance understanding of MTS properties in military environments.

AN EXEMPLAR RESEARCH PROGRAM ON ORIGINS AND CONSEQUENCES OF MULTITEAM PROPERTIES

Teams are the basic unit of work in the Army, often forming a complex "team of teams" (Mathieu et al., 2001; Zaccaro et al., 2012). Teams consist of two or more individuals who interact interdependently toward the accomplishment of shared goals (Kozlowski and Ilgen, 2006). Individuals who work in such organizational forms face the added complexity of managing information and relationships within a large collective. These individuals are also affected by the cognitive, affective, and motivational properties of both their immediate teams and the MTS. Recent research on between-team processes has found evidence of countervailing forces whereby these processes can have both positive and negative consequences for system functioning (DeChurch and Zaccaro, 2013; Lanaj et al., 2013). Whereas MTS research is at a relatively early stage, given the team-based structure of the Army, exploratory research on MTSs seems promising.

The committee's recommended research agenda addresses three questions relevant to MTS functioning in the context of military environments:

1. What are the underlying generative mechanisms that explain how properties come about in MTSs (i.e., between component teams and at the system level)?
2. What are the consequences of different degrees and patterns of properties in MTSs?
3. What are some interventions through which properties can be shaped or reshaped to optimally regulate individual and team behavior and maximize MTS functioning?

To assist ARI to answer these questions, the committee outlines below five potential phases of research, leveraging multiple methodologies, that ARI may find useful in developing a research program to answer these questions.

Phase 1: Primary Data Collection

The first step of this potential research program is to gather a large sample of data on MTSs that include information about MTS compositional attributes (e.g., diversity of component teams, degree to which individuals and teams have prior relationships); multilevel properties; and individual, team, and MTS outcomes. The goal of this phase of the research would be to provide important inputs for later developments such as an agent-based model (phase 2) and the virtual experiments described in phase 4. Data collections that would be useful are similar to those conducted in U.S. Air Force officer training programs that have been used in the research reported by Davison and colleagues (2012) and Lanaj and colleagues (2013). These data sets follow military personnel as they cycle through an MTS training exercise. Such data are well suited to the research program proposed here for the Army because they afford a substantial amount of researcher control while also affording some generalizability to the population of interest.

Ideally, data for this proposed program would be gathered as part of the longitudinal survey data collection described in Chapter 7. That chapter details a proposed cohort study for which samples of soldiers will be tracked over time. It would not only sample individual soldiers but would also include sampling of the squads and platoons to which they belong at each data collection time point. This sampling strategy would provide measures of team, between-team, and MTS properties, gathered longitudinally to enable sequential, time-based analyses to be conducted. Studying the development of MTS properties would allow the identification of thresholds: critical points where a pattern of interaction among team members crystallizes into an MTS property such as cohesion, trust, or a shared mental model. These studies would also allow the identification of critical phase transitions that mark important developmental cycles of the MTS as it grows from nascence to a mature system.

Phase 2: Agent-Based Model of MTS Generative Mechanisms

The second phase of this potential research program to study MTSs includes conceptual development where there is existing theory, combined with agent-based modeling. The conceptual work would use existing research to detail the generative mechanisms through which individuals' actions and interactions ultimately give rise to MTS properties. To inform this phase, the committee suggests using prior research on team emergence (Kozlowski and Chao, 2012; Kozlowski et al., 2013; Klein and Kozlowski, 2000) to specify the generative mechanisms (Epstein, 1999) that give rise to emergent affective, cognitive, and motivational properties in teams, between teams, and at the MTS level. The primary data collected in phase 1 would then be used to fit the model. In an agent-based model, the generative mechanisms are the microprocesses through which an actor's (i.e., an individual's) thought, feeling, motive, or behavior comes about. Agent-based modeling has been advanced as particularly useful for understanding social context in the area of networks (National Research Council, 2008; Harrison et al., 2007; Monge and Contractor, 2003; Palazzolo et al., 2006) and teams (Ilgen and Hulin, 2000), although existing applications to teams have been rare (see Kuljanin, 2011, for a notable exception).

The goal of this research phase is to generate a model that can then be used to run virtual experiments (see phase 4). Given the high cost of experimenting on intact MTSs, the committee encourages the use of virtual experiments prior to experimentation with human groups in order to ensure that important treatment conditions are identified efficiently and to hasten the discovery of important aspects of context that stem from MTS properties.

Phase 3: Linking MTS Properties to Outcomes

In the third phase of this exemplar research program, all available primary data would be used to identify the precise relationships between MTS properties and outcomes. Setting up a centralized open data repository for MTS research would greatly facilitate this research phase. The goal of phase 3 is to identify which levels, types, and patterns of properties optimize outcomes (i.e., maximize the benefits of the MTS state while minimizing its adverse effects) at multiple levels.

The analyses to support this goal can be informed by two ideas from complexity thinking (Anderson, 1999; Byrne, 2002). First is the notion that properties may have both positive and negative consequences. This is often the case for consequences of properties at different levels of analysis. For example, an MTS property that is beneficial for the team may be harmful for the system. Another example is an MTS property, such as cohesion, that buffers the team from poor morale but also increases the likelihood that members will engage in and condone problem behaviors (Narayanan et al., 2006; Pearsall and Ellis, 2011). The second theme informed by complexity theory is that relations in an MTS are likely to be nonlinear and interactive. For example, the effects of MTS cohesion on problem behaviors depend in part on the strength of MTS efficacy.

Phase 4: Identifying Levers for MTS Properties

In phase 4 of the exemplar MTS research program, the relationships identified in phase 3 could be used to design a series of virtual experiments run with computer-simulated MTSs. For example, the desired patterns of MTS properties identified in phase 3 could be used as criteria in the virtual experiments. In each of a series of model runs, the researchers adjust initial conditions of the MTS compositional attributes and then run the agent-based model under those conditions for thousands of MTSs, watching the development of MTS properties at different levels. The goal of virtual experiments would be to identify the conditions under which the optimal configurations of MTS properties come about, so that efficient experimentation can proceed. The committee cautions that virtual experiments should not replace research on actual soldiers in real military environments, but virtual experiments serve as a mechanism to develop and test hypotheses and methodologies to develop targeted and valid research programs to apply in the field where time and access is more severely limited.

Phase 5: Causally Shaping MTS Properties

As the final phase of this exemplar MTS research program, the committee suggests ARI could use the outputs of phase 4 to design experimental manipulations of MTS design features (i.e., compositional attributes) to test in an "MTS laboratory." In this carefully monitored but real-world setting, relevantly similar MTSs would be randomly assigned to operate under different conditions so that effects on MTS properties can be measured in real human groups, ultimately with real soldiers in actual military environments (to include training environments). These controlled experiments are necessary to establish causality of the interventions suggested in the virtual experiments and to ensure that the causal effects indeed generalize (Cook and Campbell, 1976) from the simulated MTSs to human MTSs.

Conclusion on the Exemplar MTS Research Program

The context of military environments is largely shaped by the design of work in teams and systems of teams (Goodwin et al., 2012). The identification of properties in MTSs is one area where MTS research can improve understanding of the specific aspects of military context that shape soldiers actions and interactions. The most valuable research on MTSs will incorporate complexity thinking (Anderson, 1999; Byrne, 2002) and triangulate computational methods with more traditional social science methods. An MTS research program will need to leverage an interdisciplinary team of traditional social scientists (e.g., psychologists, sociologists, anthropologists) working alongside computationally intensive scientists (e.g., industrial engineers, computational social scientists; see Lazer et al., 2009). This multimethod approach to the study of MTS properties can provide valuable insight into how MTS properties arise, the consequences of those properties, and effective interventions to regulate collective properties at multiple levels.

FUTURE RESEARCH ON MULTITEAM SYSTEMS

Conclusion 6
The committee concludes that the teams and multiteam systems within

which individuals work constitute an important source of context for the behavior of individuals and small units in military environments.

Recommendation 6
The U.S. Army Research Institute for the Behavioral and Social Sciences and other U.S. military funding agencies should support basic research that identifies:

1. **how actions and interactions among individuals give rise to properties such as cohesion in teams, between teams, and in systems of teams;**
2. **the positive and negative consequences of these properties on individuals, teams, and multiteam systems; and**
3. **effective interventions such as leadership that can be used to regulate these properties.**

REFERENCES

Anderson, P. (1999). Perspective: Complexity theory and organization science. *Organization Science*, 10(3):216-232.

Byrne, D. (2002). *Complexity Theory and the Social Sciences: An Introduction*. London and New York: Routledge.

Cook, T.D., and D.T. Campbell. (1976). The design and conduct of quasi-experiments and true experiments in field settings. In M.D. Dunnette, Ed., *Handbook of Industrial and Organizational Psychology*. Chicago, IL: Rand McNally College Publication.

Costa, A.C. (2003). Work team trust and effectiveness. *Personnel Review*, 32(5):605-622.

Cronin, M.A., L.R. Weingart, and G. Todorova. (2011). Dynamics in groups: Are we there yet? *The Academy of Management Annals*, 5(1):571-612.

Curseu, P.L. (2006). Emergent states in virtual teams: A complex adaptive systems perspective. *Journal of Information Technology*, 21(4):249-261.

Davison, R.B., J.R. Hollenbeck, C.M. Barnes, D.J. Sleesman, and D.R. Ilgen. (2012). Coordinated action in multiteam systems. *Journal of Applied Psychology*, 97(4):808-824.

DeChurch, L.A., and M.A. Marks. (2006). Leadership in multiteam systems. *Journal of Applied Psychology*, 91(2):311-329.

DeChurch, L.A., and J.E. Mathieu. (2009). Thinking in terms of multiteam systems. In G.F. Goodwin and C.S. Burke, Eds., *Team Effectiveness in Complex Organizations: Cross-disciplinary Perspectives and Approaches* (pp. 267-292). New York: Routledge.

DeChurch, L.A., and J.R. Mesmer-Magnus. (2010). The cognitive underpinnings of effective teamwork: A meta-analysis. *Journal of Applied Psychology*, 95(1):32-53.

DeChurch, L.A., and S.J. Zaccaro. (2010). Perspectives: Teams won't solve this problem. *Human Factors: The Journal of the Human Factors and Ergonomics Society*, 52(2):329-334.

DeChurch, L.A., and S.J. Zaccaro. (2013). *Innovation in scientific multiteam systems: Confluent and countervailing forces*. Paper presented at the July 1, 2013, National Academy of Sciences, National Research Council, Workshop on Science Team Dynamics and Effectiveness. Available: http://sites.nationalacademies.org/DBASSE/BBCSS/DBASSE_083679 [accessed April 2014].

DeChurch, L.A., C.S. Burke, M.L. Shuffler, R. Lyons, D. Doty, and E. Salas. (2011). A historiometric analysis of leadership in mission critical multiteam environments. *The Leadership Quarterly,* 22(1):152-169.

DeChurch, L.A., J.R. Mesmer-Magnus, and D. Doty. (2013). Moving beyond relationship and task conflict: Toward a process-state perspective. *Journal of Applied Psychology,* 98(4):559-578.

De Jong, B.A., and T. Elfring. (2010). How does trust affect the performance of ongoing teams? The mediating role of reflexivity, monitoring, and effort. *Academy of Management Journal,* 53(3):535-549.

Department of the Army. (2011). *Military Operations: Army Force Generation.* Army Regulation 525-29. Washington, DC: Headquarters, Department of the Army. Available: http://www.forscom.army.mil/graphics/r525_29.pdf [April 2014].

DiRosa, G.A. (2013). *Emergent Phenomena in Multiteam Systems: An Examination of Between-Team Cohesion* (Doctoral dissertation, George Mason University). Available: http://digilib.gmu.edu/dspace/handle/1920/8239 [May 2014].

Edmondson, A. (1999). Psychological safety and learning behavior in work teams. *Administrative Science Quarterly,* 44(2):350-383.

Ellis, A.P. (2006). System breakdown: The role of mental models and transactive memory in the relationship between acute stress and team performance. *Academy of Management Journal,* 49(3):576-589.

Epstein, J.M. (1999). Agent-based computational models and generative social science. *Complexity,* 4(5):41-60.

Festinger, L. (1950). Informal social communication. *Psychological Review,* 57(5):271-282.

Gersick, C.J., and Hackman, J.R. (1990). Habitual routines in task-performing groups. *Organizational behavior and human decision processes,* 47(1):65-97.

Goodwin, G.F., P.J.M.D. Essens, and D. Smith. (2012). Multiteam systems in the public sector. In S.J. Zaccaro, M.A. Marks, and L. DeChurch, Eds., *Multiteam Systems: An Organization Form for Dynamic and Complex Environments* (pp. 53-79). New York: Routledge Academic.

Gully, S.M., K.A. Incalcaterra, A. Joshi, and J.M. Beaubien. (2002). A meta-analysis of team-efficacy, potency, and performance: Interdependence and level of analysis as moderators of observed relationships. *Journal of Applied Psychology,* 87(5):819-832.

Harrison, J.R., Z. Lin, G.R. Carroll, and K.M. Carley. (2007). Simulation modeling in organizational and management research. *Academy of Management Review,* 32(4):1,229-1,245.

Hogg, M.A., and D.I. Terry. (2000). Social identity and self-categorization processes in organizational contexts. *Academy of Management Review,* 25(1):121-140.

Ilgen, D.R., and C.L. Hulin, Eds. (2000). *Computational Modeling of Behavior in Organizations: The Third Scientific Discipline.* Washington, DC: American Psychological Association.

Jimenez-Rodriguez, M. (2012). *Two Pathways to Performance: Affective- and Motivationally-Driven Development in Virtual Multiteam Systems.* (Doctoral dissertation, University of Central Florida). Available: http://etd.fcla.edu/CF/CFE0004389/Jimenez_Miliani_201207_PhD.pdf [May 2014].

Klein, K.J., and S.W.J. Kozlowski. (2000). From micro to meso: Critical steps in conceptualizing and conducting multilevel research. *Organizational Research Methods,* 3(3):211-236.

Kozlowski, S.W.J., and G.T. Chao. (2012). The dynamics of emergence: Cognition and cohesion in work teams. *Managerial and Decision Economics,* 33(5-6):335-354.

Kozlowski, S.W.J., and D.R. Ilgen. (2006). Enhancing the effectiveness of work groups and teams. *Psychological Science in the Public Interest,* 7(3):77-124.

Kozlowski, S.W.J., G.T. Chao, J.A. Grand, M.T. Braun, and G. Kujanin. (2013). Advancing multilevel research design: Capturing the dynamics of emergence. *Organizational Research Methods,* 16(4):581-615.

Kuljanin, G. (2011). *A Computational Study of Team Collaboration and Performance.* (Doctoral dissertation, Michigan State University). Available: http://etd.lib.msu.edu/islandora/object/etd%3A645/datastream/OBJ/view [March 2014].

Lanaj, K., J. Hollenbeck, D. Ilgen, C. Barnes, and S. Harmon. (2013). The double-edged sword of decentralized planning in multiteam systems. *Academy of Management Journal,* 56(3):735-757.

Lazer, D., A.S. Pentland, L. Adamic, S. Aral, A.L. Barabasi, D. Brewer, N. Christakis, N. Contractor, J. Fowler, M. Gutmann, T. Jebara, G. King, M. Macy, D. Roy, and M. Van Alstyne. (2009). Life in the network: The coming age of computational social science. *Science*, 323(5915):721-723.

Lewis, K. (2003). Measuring transactive memory systems in the field: Scale development and validation. *Journal of Applied Psychology*, 88(4):587-604.

Marks, M.A., J.E. Mathieu, and S.J. Zaccaro. (2001). A temporally based framework and taxonomy of team processes. *Academy of Management Review*, 26(3):356-376.

Marks, M.A., L.A. DeChurch, J.E. Mathieu, F.J. Panzer, and A. Alonso. (2005). Teamwork in multiteam systems. *Journal of Applied Psychology*, 90(5):964-971.

Mathieu, J.E., T.S. Heffner, G.F. Goodwin, E. Salas, and J.A. Cannon-Bowers. (2000). The influence of shared mental models on team process and performance. *Journal of Applied Psychology*, 85(2):273-283.

Mathieu, J.E., M.A. Marks, and S.J. Zaccaro. (2001). Multi-team systems. *International Handbook of Work and Organizational Psychology*, 2:289-313.

Mayer, R.C., J.H. Davis, and F.D. Schoorman. (1995). An integrative model of organizational trust. *Academy of Management Review*, 20(3):709-734.

Monge, P.R., and N.S. Contractor. (2003). *Theories of Communication Networks*. New York: Oxford University Press.

Mullen, B., and C. Copper. (1994). The relation between group cohesiveness and performance: An integration. *Psychological Bulletin*, 115(2):210-227.

Narayanan, J., S. Ronson, and M.M. Pillutla. (2006). Groups as enablers of unethical behavior: The role of cohesion on group member actions. *Research on Managing Groups and Teams*, 8:127-147.

National Research Council. (2008). *Behavioral Modeling and Simulation: From Individuals to Societies.* Committee on Organizational Modeling: From Individuals to Societies, G.L. Zacharias, J. MacMillian, and S. Van Hemel, Eds. Board on Behavioral, Cognitive, and Sensory Sciences, Division of Behavioral and Social Sciences and Education. Washington, DC: The National Academies Press.

Palazzolo, E.T., D.A Serb, Y. She, C. Su, and N.S. Contractor. (2006). Coevolution of communication and knowledge networks in transactive memory systems: Using computational models for theoretical development. *Communication Theory*, 16(2):223-250.

Pearsall, M.J., and A.P Ellis. (2011). Thick as thieves: The effects of ethical orientation and psychological safety on unethical team behavior. *Journal of Applied Psychology*, 96(2):401-411.

Whyte, G. (1993). Escalating commitment in individual and group decision making: A prospect theory approach. *Organizational Behavior and Human Decision Processes,* 54(3):430-455.

Zaccaro, S.J., M.A. Marks, and L.A. DeChurch, Eds. (2012). *Multiteam Systems: An Organization Form for Dynamic and Complex Environments*. New York: Routledge.

Zhang, Z.-X., P.S. Hempel, Y.L. Han, and D. Tjosvold. (2007). Transactive memory system links work team characteristics and performance. *Journal of Applied Psychology,* 92(6):1,722-1,730.

7

Longitudinal Survey Data for Empirical Research on Military Environments

Researchers need appropriate data in order to evaluate the factors that affect individual and small unit behavior in military environments. With these data, they can address questions like the following:

- What demographic, educational, and family characteristics predict a successful adjustment to military life?
- How do different family contexts and concerns shape service members' responses to particular military assignments?
- What unit-level factors affect success in the military?
- What attitudes are related to successful adjustment to military service?
- What individual-level and unit-level variables predict such undesirable events as early discharge, poor performance ratings, disciplinary actions, dysfunctional behavior (e.g., alcoholism), and suicide?
- What variables are related to poor mental health episodes among military personnel?
- How do trajectories during military service relate to readjustment after service?

In this chapter, the committee argues that these types of questions are best approached with longitudinal data, that is, repeated surveys of the same individuals over a period of years. The chapter first describes the administrative and survey data that are currently available about the armed forces in cross-section. It then describes many of the longitudinal surveys based on civilian populations, which could provide a model for an effort to collect data regarding the military. Next it presents information about the primary existing longitudinal survey conducted by the armed forces, which focuses almost exclusively on assessing service members' health. It concludes by recommending that the Department of Defense (1) collect additional administrative data from all applicants to the armed forces, (2) encourage civilian and military researchers to use the existing administrative and survey data, and (3) create a new longitudinal survey to further research on social and organizational factors in the context of military environments.

CROSS-SECTIONAL DATA ON THE MILITARY

The armed forces currently collect administrative data on the demographics, deployments, health, and performance of soldiers. In addition, they have long conducted surveys that provide information about service members in cross-section.

Administrative Data

The armed forces collect data regarding the backgrounds of applicants and recruits, which provide an overview of the military population. They currently collect data on geographic origin, race, age, test scores, education, and gender. While these data provide important information on the contexts from which service members come, they have not enabled researchers and policy makers to assess basic questions about the family backgrounds of recruits, which may have important implications for performance of and interactions within and between small units.

The armed forces do not, for example, gather data that would allow one to infer the socioeconomic background of applicants and service members. Since at least the 1950s, scholars have tried to assess the socioeconomic backgrounds of soldiers (Mayer and Hoult, 1955). During the wars in Iraq and Afghanistan, policy makers and journalists were concerned that service members disproportionately came from poor and disadvantaged backgrounds (Rangel, 2002). Yet scholars had only one technique for using military administrative data to draw conclusions about the socioeconomic origins of recruits. They had to assess these origins based not on direct reports but rather by combining the zip code information collected by the military with the characteristics of neighborhoods (Kane, 2006). This strategy resulted in enough observations to provide statistical power to detect differences in neighborhoods of origin between service members and civilians. However, these results could reasonably be viewed as subject to the ecological fallacy: researchers incorrectly imputing the average characteristics of a geographic area to all the residents of that area. Perhaps the most famous example of this fallacy was identified in the work that first labeled it (Robinson, 1950): whereas the individual correlation between being foreign born and being illiterate was small and positive, the ecological correlation between the percent foreign born and percent illiterate by region in the United States was large and negative.

Surveys

The history of large-scale, cross-sectional surveys conducted by the U.S. military stretches back at least to the American Soldier studies that were directed by Samuel Stouffer during World War II. This series of cross-sectional surveys was administered to nearly half a million service members during the course of that war. In the late 1940s, the results were published in multiple volumes that contributed much to our understanding of military life (e.g., Stouffer, 1949a, 1949b) and produced important concepts such as the theory of relative deprivation (Sewell, 1989). The surveys themselves also helped refine survey methodology (Stouffer, 1966).

The Department of Defense continues to conduct surveys that address the same topics, and these surveys are primarily cross-sectional. Civilian researchers have used the Survey of Active Duty Military Personnel, for example, to generate insight into questions about the relationships between military and civilian society. Some scholars have used the 1999 version of that survey to examine whether gender and race moderate work satisfaction in the military (Lundquist, 2008), as well as to evaluate the culture of particular military occupations (Burland and Lundquist, 2013).

LONGITUDINAL SURVEYS BASED ON NONMILITARY POPULATIONS

Social science research on behavior in civilian environments has long made extensive use of longitudinal surveys of samples of individuals and households, and these surveys include information on former service members. In the United States, major national surveys include multiple National Longitudinal Surveys sponsored by the Bureau of Labor Statistics, multiple surveys of school populations sponsored by the Department of Education, the Panel Study of Income Dynamics (PSID) sponsored by the National Science Foundation, the Health and Retirement Study (HRS) sponsored by the National Institute on Aging, and the National Longitudinal Study of Adolescent Health sponsored by the National Institute of Child Health and Human Development. In addition, the Census Bureau operates two large-scale, ongoing longitudinal surveys (the Survey of Income and Program Participation and the Current Population Survey) that follow waves of respondents for a year and half to four years. Other longitudinal surveys have surveyed samples of residents of American subpopulations. Notable early examples include the intergenerational Framingham Heart Study and Wisconsin Longitudinal Survey, begun in 1948 and 1957, respectively, and the National Center for Education Statistics program of longitudinal studies of factors that predict success in school (e.g., Early Childhood Longitudinal Studies).

The specifics of the existing surveys differ, but most of them share several central features, including (1) a well-designed full-probability sample designed to yield a sizable, representative sample of the population of interest, (2) a carefully constructed and pretested questionnaire intended to yield useful evidence on personal backgrounds and behaviors, and (3) periodic reinterviews of respondents aiming to trace the dynamics of their circumstances and outcomes over time. Longitudinal surveys with these features have proved to be enormously valuable resources for description of civilian work, health, education, and family experiences. They have provided essential data for studies of the determinants of individual and household behaviors, fertility decisions, success in the labor force, and cognitive achievements in school. They have facilitated research aiming to distinguish causal effects from statistical associations. It is difficult to imagine modern empirical social science without them.

Civilian longitudinal surveys are rarely based on simple random samples of the population but usually follow stratified random sampling strategies in order to generate information both about individuals and about the groups of which they are part. For example, the National Longitudinal Survey of 1979 sampled housing units and then, within those units, sampled individuals between the ages of 14 and 21. In some cases, the sample contains multiple siblings in the same family, the data for which have been used, for example, to estimate family fixed effects models (Rosenzweig and Wolpin, 1995). As another example, the High School and Beyond survey of 1980 sampled first schools and then students from within those schools. This complex structure has enabled researchers to conduct analyses both on individuals and on groups. For example, researchers have examined how educational opportunities vary both between and within schools (Gamoran, 1987).

Survey coordinators have encouraged scholars to use the data from the large longitudinal civilian surveys, such as the PSID and the National Longitudinal Surveys, by convening conferences that focus on early results. In 2005, for example, the PSID project staff convened a conference for researchers using the data from the newly launched Child Development Supplement of that survey. At such conferences, scholars benefit from having a venue to present findings and receive critiques and suggestions from other researchers who have experience using the same data.

Because they represent the entire American population, many of the existing longitudinal surveys include some respondents who have served in the armed forces. Social scientists have occasionally used the available data to compare the labor-market, health, and other outcomes of persons who have or have not performed military service. They have used several of these national longitudinal studies to evaluate outcomes related to the military, though they have assessed such phenomena not during military service but afterward among veterans.

Scholars have most often evaluated questions related to military service using the National Longitudinal Surveys' National Longitudinal Survey of Youth 1979 (NLSY79). When it was first fielded, the NLSY79 included an oversample of 1,280 people serving in the armed forces in 1978 who had been born between 1957 and 1961. This oversample was conducted in two stages, with the first stage drawing a sample of 200 military "units."[1] In the second stage, individuals within these units were sampled based on their birth years, with oversampling to include enough women in the military sample. The sample was also stratified on the basis of military branch and geographic location. In principle, one could use this sample to estimate "unit" level behavior, though apparently no research has done this. Unfortunately, 84 percent of the oversample was dropped in the 1985 NLSY79 administration. Yet in the first year and the years after the survey began, 552 male respondents enlisted in the armed forces but were not technically included in this oversample. After 1985, therefore, the NLSY79 has continued to follow 756 men who have served in the military. A significant body of work examines how these NLSY79 veterans fare according to at least four different types of outcomes: labor market (MacLean and Parsons, 2010; Teachman and Tedrow, 2007), health (Teachman, 2011), marital status (Lundquist, 2006), and crime (Bouffard, 2005).

Researchers have recently also begun to use the HRS to examine the long-term impacts of service among the population that served at least 40 years ago. The HRS is a panel survey that was started in 1992; it features a representative national probability sample of the U.S. population who were 50 years of age or older in 1992. Since that time, the survey has added subsequent cohorts to reach a sample of more than 20,000 older people. Because rates of service in older cohorts were much higher than they are today (due to the earlier presence of the draft, which may make some of the findings not generalizable to members of the military in an all-volunteer force), the sample includes a relatively large share of veterans. Approximately 50 percent of the male HRS respondents have served in the

[1]The frame of military units in the NLSY79 was based on Unit Identification Codes, which identified, across the services, groups of approximately 200 military personnel (roughly equivalent to an Army company) assigned to the same geographic location.

military. Researchers have used these data to explore questions regarding health and mortality after service (London and Wilmoth, 2006; MacLean and Edwards, 2010; Wilmoth et al., 2010).

Scholars have recently begun to use the Adolescent Health Survey (Add Health) to examine how people come to enlist in the armed forces. This survey consists of a random sample of 20,745 students in grades 7-12 in 1994-1995. Add Health includes some questions regarding military service and deployment. These data have also been linked to military administrative records. Researchers have used them to assess pathways into military service (Burdette et al., 2009; Wang et al., 2012). By the 2008 wave of the survey, approximately 12 percent of the men had enlisted in the military. Rates of service among women were less than 3 percent (Wang et al., 2012).

Researchers have also evaluated the socioeconomic characteristics of recruits by using civilian surveys (U.S. Congressional Budget Office, 2007). This research is limited because these surveys typically include relatively small numbers of military recruits from which to generalize. For example, the U.S. Congressional Budget Office draws on the National Longitudinal Survey of Youth 1997, which is a survey of youth born between 1980 and 1984 and has information on only approximately 100 enlistees (U.S. Congressional Budget Office, 2007).[2]

Research using these civilian-based surveys has been limited in two important ways. First, the numbers of respondents with military backgrounds are relatively small and the questions posed do not focus on their military experiences. Hence, existing surveys do not provide the foundation for systematic study of behavior in military environments. Second, these civilian-based surveys are, by definition, limited to particular cohorts. The HRS, for example, contains data contributed by people who were first eligible to serve in the military in the decades prior to and including the early 1970s. The NLSY79 includes information about people who began their military service in the late 1970s and early 1980s. Add Health represents people who became eligible to serve in the armed forces in the late 1990s.

THE MILLENNIUM COHORT STUDY: A LONGITUDINAL SURVEY BASED ON THE MILITARY POPULATION

The Department of Defense has been operating a large-scale longitudinal study since 2001, the Millennium Cohort Study (developed in response

[2]"The NLSY sample draws disproportionately from the lower end of the income distribution. CBO [Congressional Budget Office] weighted the full sample to represent U.S. households with children in residence. As a result, the characteristics of the military subset of that sample should be representative of young enlisted personnel in 2000. Because of the ages of the young people included in the NLSY, CBO's sample did not contain any military officers" (U.S. Congressional Budget Office, 2007, footnote 89, p. 30).

to recommendations in a 1999 report from the Institute of Medicine).[3] This survey was initiated shortly before the beginning of the wars in Iraq and Afghanistan and is focused on health outcomes. The initial web-based survey consisted of 77,047 respondents who were serving at that time (Smith and Millennium Cohort Study Team, 2009). Since 2001, the survey has added three more panels of random samples of people serving in each of three subsequent years: 2004, 2007, and 2011.[4] Millennium cohort respondents complete a survey every 3 years and continue to do so after leaving service. The survey data are linked to multiple administrative datasets, including information from, among many others, medical history, mortality, and deployment data (Smith and Millennium Cohort Study Team, 2009). In 2011, the survey added a family component with a goal of incorporating 10,000 family members. The goal is to have a total of approximately 200,000 respondents. The study will continue through 2022. The study design does not appear to contain a plan to add cohorts after the most recent wave in 2011 or to continue the survey past the projected end date of 2022.

The survey is primarily focused on health outcomes. It is designed to elicit information about military experiences, health outcomes, and health care (Smith and the Millennium Cohort Study Team, 2009). The questionnaire for the population serving in 2010, for example, consists of 99 questions, the majority of which concern health conditions. Many of the questions are quite detailed. One question asks, for example, if the respondent has ever been diagnosed with any of 46 different conditions, along with the year of diagnosis, as well as whether the respondent was hospitalized. Data obtained in these periodic surveys of respondents are linked with their Department of Defense administrative records, which enables research that effectively uses both data sources. The administrative records include demographic information regarding race, gender, and age.

As would be expected based on the survey's focus on health, the data have primarily been used in research regarding health outcomes (Jacobson et al., 2012), but they have also been used to study sexual harassment (LeardMann et al., 2013) and civilian employment (Horton et al., 2013). The study recently added a family component, which will provide essential

[3]The Department of Defense also operates, along with the National Institute of Mental Health, another shorter-term epidemiologic study (5-year study to complete in 2014) that includes pre- and postdeployment surveys focused on suicide: the Army Study to Assess Risk and Resilience in Servicemembers (STARRS). The STARRS study team includes researchers from the Uniformed Services University of the Health Sciences; University of California, San Diego; University of Michigan; Harvard Medical School; and the National Institute of Health. For more information, see http://www.armystarrs.org/ [January 2014].

[4]Information about the Millennium Cohort Study available: http://www.millenniumcohort.org/aboutstudy.php [March 2014].

information on the family context that shapes service members' behavior and outcomes.

The data do not, however, appear to include crucial information for determining the impact of social and organizational factors on the context of military environments. They do not, for example, provide information about service members' social origins, such as parental socioeconomic status and educational attainment.

The Millennium Cohort Study is available in principle to all researchers but has been little used outside the survey team. Currently, the majority of the publications that are listed as using this survey have been written by project staff.

CREATION OF A LONGITUDINAL DATABASE

The committee was struck by the potential utility of vast amounts of administrative and survey data that are currently collected by multiple entities within the Department of Defense, but are not retained or maintained in such a way as to facilitate exploratory research programs reliant upon such data. Therefore, the committee advocates the creation of a longitudinal database to store already collected administrative and survey data and to be expanded to include data from the new longitudinal survey described below. The database should capture as wide a range of administrative and survey data as possible, to include, for example, responses from surveys given across the armed services, results of initial testing, individual demographics and biodata, duty rotations, assignments, positions, and performance evaluations. It should also facilitate unit-level research (see Chapter 6) by correlating individual and unit-level data. In short, any data pertaining to a soldier's development, performance, and progress should be tracked and integrated. Establishing a central repository for data collected from a probability sample of all recruits (with data providing a record of career paths and achievements for recruits from all backgrounds) would facilitate combining sets of data to provide a record of career paths and achievements for recruits from all backgrounds. Consistent with Recommendation 1, the database would serve as the access point for making large amounts of appropriate data available to internal and external behavioral researchers to study basic scientific questions in military contexts. While the committee recognizes that confidentiality concerns and external access issues will need to be addressed, the implementation of such a database would provide an unprecedented collection of data to benefit basic understanding of the impact of social and organizational factors on the behaviors of individuals and groups in the context of military environments. The committee also recognizes that the creation and maintenance of such a database would require funding beyond that required for data collection.

A LONGITUDINAL SURVEY

Conclusion 7
The committee concludes that the Army does not currently collect or distribute sufficient data necessary to answer future questions about how social and organizational factors affect the behavior of individuals and small units.

As mentioned above, scholars and policy makers have long expressed interest in the socioeconomic characteristics of recruits, but have not been able to address such basic questions with existing administrative data (U.S. Congressional Budget Office, 2007; Mayer and Hoult, 1955). If the necessary data were collected, researchers could use them to specify how family background correlates with how service members behave and interact. For example, the armed forces could collect information about the socioeconomic characteristics of parents, such as parental occupational and educational attainments. They could also collect other standard demographic data, such as marital status, based on advice from military and civilian researchers. These data would enable researchers to compare the characteristics of recruits to those of the larger population as reflected in the Decennial Census, the Current Population Survey, and other civilian longitudinal studies. Such data could then be linked to other administrative records, as well as being linked with the information collected under the survey proposed below.

Recommendation 7.1
The U.S. military should collect more demographic and socioeconomic information about potential recruits than it currently does in the application process.

Research on social and organizational factors in the context of military environments could also be advanced more quickly if civilian researchers were able to use the existing data more easily. According to a summary of a recent report by a study committee of the Institute of Medicine (Office of News and Public Information, National Academies, 2013):[5]

> Due to limited access to data and the scarcity of research focusing on economic, social, and other impacts of deployment on military service members and their families, the committee was unable to answer many questions about the readjustment needs of this population and the status and effectiveness of support programs. A large array of relevant data are being collected by several federal departments and agencies, and if it were

[5]See Institute of Medicine (2013).

possible to fully link and integrate this data, the aggregated information could be comprehensively analyzed to answer many key questions about readjustment, the committee said. However, numerous barriers hinder access to this data, the committee found, such as unclear procedures and steps for making data requests.

Recommendation 7.2
The U.S. Army Research Institute for the Behavioral and Social Sciences and other U.S. military funding agencies should work with project staff of the Millennium Cohort Study and with other relevant parties collecting survey and administrative data on military personnel to:

1. **create a longitudinal database to be composed of survey data and administrative records presently collected and data from future surveys that may be administered to military personnel;**
2. **fund and disseminate research using the survey data and administrative records collected by the Department of Defense; and**
3. **convene, support, and publicize conferences for researchers who are currently using this data or who are interested in using this data for future research.**

Through the process outlined in this recommendation, the data would become more widely available to all researchers, and the initiative should also incorporate funding for outside researchers.

The Millennium Cohort Study has proven to be a rich source of data regarding the health of service members, yet it is not designed to elicit information about a wider array of topics of potential interest to the U.S. Army Research Institute for the Behavioral and Social Sciences or the Department of Defense. Furthermore, its activity is planned to end in 2022, with no new cohorts after 2011, and it does not contain the necessary information that would enable researchers to address directly the topics explored in this report, such as norms (Chapter 2), status in small units (Chapter 5), and multiteam systems (Chapter 6). While the committee deliberated whether a continuation of the Millennium Cohort Study would be satisfactory for these needs, the committee determined that it would not (due partly to its focus on health outcomes and partly to its planned termination but also to its focus on the individual soldier, a focus that does not include sufficient attention to unit-level measures). To evaluate the topics of research recommended in this report, the Department of Defense should launch a new longitudinal study as recommended below. This study will require substantial effort, and execution will require considerable resources. The committee believes the Department of Defense should seek assistance in developing such a study to move it ahead effectively and expeditiously, and the new survey should draw on the substantial experience of past civilian longitudinal surveys and of the Millennium Cohort Study, as appropriate.

Recommendation 7.3
The U.S. Army Research Institute for the Behavioral and Social Sciences should establish a working group of experts in survey research, empirical social science, and military subject matter charged with development of a new longitudinal survey strategy to track both individuals and small units over time.

In addition to developing the new longitudinal survey, the working group would be charged with assessing the number of times an average active service member has to respond to surveys and, if the number is deemed excessive, suggesting ways to minimize these instances.

To be most useful, the target population should encompass all new recruits (both officers and enlisted personnel), with the baseline interview undertaken near each recruit's time of entry into the armed forces. However, the design of the study's starting point should consider how to capture data descriptive of entire existing units (as required for research on multiteam systems, as discussed in Chapter 6) and thereby allow for sampling soldiers by organizational level. While some stratified probability sample of new recruits would become members of the sample, additional soldiers further along in their careers would likely need to be adopted into the survey sample. The stratification could reflect both the characteristics of the units they join and individual background characteristics (such as prior educational attainments). As in the current sample design, respondents would subsequently be interviewed periodically throughout the duration of their service, as well as afterward. To facilitate study of contextual determinants of behavior, consideration should be given to supplementary data collection aiming to characterize the environments within which military respondents act. In addition, the survey data should be linked to administrative data to provide information on success in the military. To give just two examples, survey responses of respondents could be linked to their records of promotions and honors.

REFERENCES

Bouffard, L.A. (2005). The military as a bridging environment in criminal careers: Differential outcomes of the military experience. *Armed Forces and Society,* 31(2):273-295.

Burdette, A.M., V.E. Wang, G.H. Elder, T.D. Hill, and J. Benson. (2009). Serving God and country? Religious involvement and military service among young adult men. *Journal for the Scientific Study of Religion,* 48(4):794-804.

Burland, D., and J.H. Lundquist. (2013). The dynamic lives and static institutions of the "Two Armies": Data from the survey of active duty personnel. *Armed Forces and Society,* 39(1):78-101.

Gamoran, A. (1987). The stratification of high school learning opportunities. *Sociology of Education,* 60(3):135-155.

Horton, J.L., I.G. Jacobson, C.A. Wong, T.S. Wells, E.J. Boyko, B. Smith, M.A. Ryan, T.C. Smith, and Millennium Cohort Study Team. (2013). The impact of prior deployment experience on civilian employment after military service. *Occupational and Environmental Medicine,* 70(6):408-417.

Institute of Medicine. (1999). *Gulf War Veterans: Measuring Health.* L.M. Hernandez, J.S. Durch, D.G. Blazer II, and I.V. Hoverman, Eds.; Committee on Measuring the Health of Gulf War Veterans, Institute of Medicine. Washington, DC: The National Academies Press.

Institute of Medicine. (2013). *Returning Home from Iraq and Afghanistan: Assessment of Readjustment Needs of Veterans, Service Members, and Their Families.* Committee on the Initial Assessment of Readjustment Needs of Military Personnel, Veterans, and Their Families. Board on the Health of Select Populations. Washington, DC: The National Academies Press.

Jacobson, I.G., J.L. Horton, C.A. LeardMann, M.A.K. Ryan, E.J. Boyko, T.S. Wells, B. Smith, and T.C. Smith. (2012). Posttraumatic stress disorder and depression among U.S. military health care professionals deployed in support of operations in Iraq and Afghanistan. *Journal of Traumatic Stress,* 25(6):616-623.

Kane, T. (2006). *Who Are the Recruits? The Demographic Characteristics of U.S. Military Enlistment, 2003-2005.* Washington, DC: Heritage Foundation.

LeardMann, C.A., A. Pietrucha, K.M. Magruder, B. Smith, M. Murdoch, I.G. Jacobson, M.A.K. Ryan, G. Gackstetter, T.C. Smith, and Millenium Cohort Study Team. (2013). Combat deployment is associated with sexual harassment or sexual assault in a large, female military cohort. *Women's Health Issues,* 23(4):e215-e223. Available: http://www.whijournal.com/article/S1049-3867(13)00038-8/fulltext [April 2014].

London, A.S., and J.M. Wilmoth. (2006). Military service and (dis)continuity in the life course: Evidence on disadvantage and mortality from the health and retirement study and the study of assets and health dynamics among the oldest-old. *Research on Aging,* 28(1):135-159.

Lundquist, J.H. (2006). The black-white gap in marital dissolution among young adults: What can a counterfactual scenario tell us? *Social Problems,* 53(3):421-441.

Lundquist, J.H. (2008). Ethnic and gender satisfaction in the military: The effect of a meritocratic institution. *American Sociological Review,* 73(3):477-496.

MacLean, A., and R.D. Edwards. (2010). The pervasive role of rank in the health of U.S. veterans. *Armed Forces and Society,* 36(5):765-785.

MacLean, A., and N.L. Parsons. (2010). Unequal risk: Combat occupations in the volunteer military. *Sociological Perspectives,* 53(3):347-372.

Mayer, A.J., and T.F. Hoult. (1955). Social stratification and combat survival. *Social Forces,* 34(2):155-159.

Office of News and Public Information, The National Academies. (2013, March 26). *For Immediate Release: Evidence-Based Diagnostics and Therapies and Long-Term Forecasts of Needs Among Steps Necessary to Ease Iraq and Afghanistan Service Members' Readjustment to Post-Deployment Life.* News Release. Washington, DC: The National Academies. Available: http://www8.nationalacademies.org/onpinews/newsitem.aspx?RecordID=13499 [June 2014].

Rangel, C.B. (2002). Bring Back the Draft. New York Times, December 31, p. A19. Available: http://www.nytimes.com/2002/12/31/opinion/bring-back-the-draft.html [April 2014].

Robinson, W.S. (1950). Ecological correlations and the behavior of individuals. *American Sociological Review,* 15(3):351-357.

Rosenzweig, M.R., and K.I. Wolpin. (1995). Sisters, siblings, and mothers: The effect of teenage childbearing on birth outcomes in a dynamic family context. *Econometrica,* 63(2):303-326.

Sewell, W.H. (1989). Some reflections on the golden-age of interdisciplinary social-psychology. *Annual Review of Sociology,* 15(1):1-16.

Smith, T.C., and Millennium Cohort Study Team. (2009). The U.S. Department of Defense Millennium Cohort Study: Career span and beyond longitudinal follow-up. *Journal of Occupational and Environmental Medicine,* 51(10):1,193-1,201.

Stouffer, S.A. (1949a). *The American Soldier: Adjustment During Army Life.* Studies in Social Pscyhology in World War II, Vol. 1. Princeton, NJ: Princeton University Press.

Stouffer, S.A. (1949b). *The American Soldier: Combat and Its Aftermath.* Studies in Social Pscyhology in World War II, Vol. 2. Princeton, NJ: Princeton University Press.

Stouffer, S.A. (1966). *Measurement and Prediction.* New York: Wiley.

Teachman, J.D. (2011). Are veterans healthier? Military service and health at age 40 in the all-volunteer-era. *Social Science Research,* 40(1):326-335.

Teachman, J.D., and L.M. Tedrow. (2007). Joining up: Did military service in the early all volunteer era affect subsequent civilian income? *Social Science Research,* 36(4):1,447-1,474.

U.S. Congressional Budget Office. (2007). *The All-Volunteer Military: Issues and Performance.* Washington, DC: U.S. Congress. Available: http://www.cbo.gov/ftpdocs/83xx/doc8313/07-19-MilitaryVol.pdf [March 2014].

Wang, L., G.H. Elder Jr., and N.J. Spence. (2012). Status configurations, military service and higher education. *Social Forces,* 91(2):397-422.

Wilmoth, J.M., A.S. London, and W.M. Parker. (2010). Military service and men's health trajectories in later life. *Journals of Gerontology Series B-Psychological Sciences and Social Sciences,* 65(6):744-755.

8

The Research Agenda: Conclusions and Recommendations

For the convenience of the reader, this chapter restates the conclusions and recommendations that were originally presented in each of the relevant report chapters and that, combined, make up the committee's recommended research agenda for the basic research program of the U.S. Army Research Institute for the Behavioral and Social Sciences (ARI). The committee recognizes that aspects of this research agenda are already under investigation by ARI and other entities, while other aspects may be in the process of being developed and implemented. Nonetheless, the committee feels it is imperative for the locus of ARI's existing work to shift from civilian settings to military settings, as discussed in the committee's first conclusion and recommendation. Furthermore, aspects of the recommended research agenda have yet to receive any research attention, and we hope these areas will develop into new research programs in the future. In considering this proposed research agenda, three key points (see Chapter 1) remain salient across the committee's conclusions and recommendations: (1) conduct basic research on soldiers at the small unit level, (2) develop unit-level measurements of social and organizational factors, and (3) develop a longitudinal survey and maintain a longitudinal database.

RELEVANT PERSONNEL

As described in Chapter 1 and reiterated as a theme carried throughout the recommendations, the committee, throughout its data-gathering process, was repeatedly struck by the lack of basic research conducted on actual soldiers within real military contexts. Although basic research is intended to provide knowledge about people and their behaviors without specific application, the committee sees a clear distinction between understanding behavior in typical military environments (as basic research) and developing specific processes or products for those environments (as applied research). The committee is convinced that the unique circumstances and challenges of military environments demand that, for basic research to be of the most benefit to the military, it must be conducted within these environments.

Conclusion 1
ARI's definition of "basic research" does not preclude scientific research on active duty soldiers in real military contexts. "Basic research is defined as systematic study directed toward a fuller knowledge or understanding of the fundamental aspects of phenomena and of observable facts without specific applications towards processes or products in mind" (U.S. Office of Management and Budget, 2013, p. 268 [p. 8 of Section 84]).

Recommendation 1
The committee strongly recommends that the Department of the Army support an appropriate mix of intramural and extramural basic scientific research on relevant Army personnel in military environments. The U.S Army Research Institute for the Behavioral and Social Sciences (ARI) should be responsible for making appropriate data on Army units available and for promoting access for both internal and external behavioral researchers to study basic scientific questions in military contexts. ARI should increase its role as a facilitator or gateway for basic behavioral research in military contexts.

NORMS

The report's second chapter, "Norms in Military Environments," describes the importance of understanding the group-level phenomena of norms, behaviors, and beliefs held in common by group members that guide behaviors and perceptions about behaviors, including whether norms are desirable or undesirable, moral, or compatible with social or organizational values or ethics. While the Army has well-defined core values, understanding the content, expression, maintenance, and development of norms over time within military contexts is a distinct and relatively untapped area of research. Norms are a critical element to a fundamental understanding of in- and out-group perceptions, normative behavior expectations, deviance, and behavior in novel situations.

Conclusion 2
The committee concludes that norms are an important dimension of the social context within small units. Due to the unique conditions of military contexts, the committee further concludes that participants in research on military norms must be active duty soldiers, if the results are to be meaningful in real military environments.

Recommendation 2
The U.S. Army Research Institute for the Behavioral and Social Sciences (ARI) and other relevant U.S. military funding agencies should fund basic research that:

1. **identifies the content of norms; the values, attitudes, and behaviors that express norms; formal and informal incentives and sanctions that maintain norms; conditions that moderate norm-relevant behavior; and the development of norms over time;**
2. **examines the relationship between norms and the performance of soldiers and the attitudes and behaviors of their leaders; and**
3. **identifies approaches for changing norms to produce more effective soldiers and units.**

To facilitate the research program on norms, the committee recommends that ARI establish a multidisciplinary task force charged with development of a program of research studying norms in military contexts.

ENVIRONMENTAL TRANSITIONS

Chapter 3, "Environmental Transitions," emphasizes the importance of understanding the effects of the regular and repeated life transitions of a military career on individuals and groups. These effects include local and specific issues of habits and routines, as well as global and generic effects such as resilience against stressors of change. Although the military is actively investigating many of these issues of concern, the dominant approach in recent and current research is from an individual and psychological perspective. In contrast, the committee believes the military would benefit tremendously from investigating environmental transitions to better understand the role, impact, and influence of the organization on the individuals and groups before, during, and after transitions.

Conclusion 3

The committee concludes that the repeated environmental transitions faced by military personnel create significant challenges and opportunities to operational effectiveness and resilience.

Recommendation 3

The U.S. Army Research Institute for the Behavioral and Social Sciences and other U.S. military funding agencies should support basic research on:

1. **individual habits and organizational routines that are disrupted by environmental transitions, including research into the positive and negative consequences of these disruptions within specific military contexts and that examines how these consequences might be proactively managed to increase unit and soldier effectiveness;**
2. **the interaction between individual characteristics and features of groups and organizations, with the aim of predicting resilience; how this interaction may differ across types of environments; and groups and organizations, as well as individuals, as the unit of analysis; and**
3. **exploring in what ways and under what conditions local disruption of habits affects global consequences for resilience.**

CONTEXTUAL LEADERSHIP

In Chapter 4, "Contextual Leadership," the committee acknowledges the enduring and extensive emphasis the military places on the value of leadership through research, training, policies, and practice. In developing future research programs, the committee believes continued efforts to understand leadership will prove valuable. To refine and focus leadership research initiatives, we suggest that such research closely examine the social context of small units, with an emphasis on the social interactions of leaders and followers at the most basic levels of military operations, the small unit.

Conclusion 4

The committee concludes that leaders play a critical role in influencing the social context, which in turn shapes positive individual behavior and effective unit performance. Understanding the social interaction of unit members and the evolving social context of the unit, to include the mutually influencing relationship between leaders and followers, is critical to effective contextual leadership in military environments.

Recommendation 4
The U.S. Army Research Institute for the Behavioral and Social Sciences and other U.S. military funding agencies should fund an agenda of basic research to identify:

1. **specific challenges to leadership created by dynamic units and systems of units over time;**
2. **leadership capabilities that support soldier adjustment to military service;**
3. **the early warning signals of undesirable behaviors and appropriate counter measures; and**
4. **how leaders can influence social interactions so as to have the most positive impact on unit performance.**

POWER AND STATUS

In the report's fifth chapter, "Distinct Sources of Power and Status in Diversified Army Units," the committee differentiates between elements of power (formal markers such as rank) and status (informal sources of social influence). While power and status are often closely aligned, misalignments can and do occur, resulting in a range of effects on both leaders and followers. Focused research initiatives to develop a fundamental understanding of the role of status in small military units will likely provide valuable insights into the behavior of individuals and groups (including members of minorities) across military environments.

Conclusion 5
The committee concludes that informal processes of negotiating status (e.g., respect and admiration from peers) are an important source of influence in small units in addition to formal power; these processes have substantial implications for human resource utilization and small unit performance.

Recommendation 5
The U.S. Army Research Institute for the Behavioral and Social Sciences and other U.S. military funding agencies should fund basic research on:

1. **how soldiers gain status;**
2. **how status attainment may differ between men and women and between combat and noncombat functions;**
3. **how the interaction between rank and status may produce positive or negative leadership outcomes; and**

4. **how status affects careers, behavioral outcomes, and small unit effectiveness.**

MULTITEAM SYSTEMS

In Chapter 6, "Multiteam Systems as the Context for Individuals and Teams," the committee acknowledges the critical importance of teams (understood broadly to include all groups of individuals working together for a common goal, including military small units) to accomplishing the military mission. Furthermore, these teams do not operate in isolation; they are just one element in a larger system that includes multiple distinct and interdependent teams. Research aimed at multiteam systems will likely result in improved understanding of focal phenomena such as trust or cohesion, as well as diffuse phenomena associated with properties such as agility and flexibility in large organizations that evolve to meet mission objectives.

Conclusion 6
The committee concludes that the teams and multiteam systems within which individuals work constitute an important source of context for the behavior of individuals and small units in military environments.

Recommendation 6
The U.S. Army Research Institute for the Behavioral and Social Sciences and other U.S. military funding agencies should support basic research that identifies:

1. **how actions and interactions among individuals give rise to properties such as cohesion in teams, between teams, and in systems of teams;**
2. **the positive and negative consequences of these properties on individuals, teams, and multiteam systems; and**
3. **effective interventions such as leadership that can be used to regulate these properties.**

LONGITUDINAL SURVEY DATA

In Chapter 7, "Longitudinal Survey Data for Empirical Research on Military Environments," the committee advocates for the collection of longitudinal data on military personnel, developed from repeated surveys of the same individuals over a period of years, to inform a multitude of research programs, including many described in Chapters 2 through 6. While a longitudinal survey is not a precondition for the development of the other studies, its parallel and simultaneous development should be a high priority. The data collected would provide unprecedented opportunities to understand prediction factors associated with adjustment and responses to military life, including career success, undesirable events, mental health, and readjustment to civilian life.

Conclusion 7
The committee concludes that the Army does not currently collect or distribute sufficient data necessary to answer future questions about how social and organizational factors affect the behavior of individuals and small units.

Recommendation 7.1
The U.S. military should collect more demographic and socioeconomic information about potential recruits than it currently does in the application process.

Recommendation 7.2
The U.S. Army Research Institute for the Behavioral and Social Sciences and other U.S. military funding agencies should work with project staff of the Millennium Cohort Study and with other relevant parties collecting survey and administrative data on military personnel to:

1. **create a longitudinal database to be composed of survey data and administrative records presently collected and data from future surveys that may be administered to military personnel;**
2. **fund and disseminate research using the survey data and administrative records collected by the Department of Defense; and**
3. **convene, support, and publicize conferences for researchers who are currently using this data or who are interested in using this data for future research.**

Recommendation 7.3
The U.S. Army Research Institute for the Behavioral and Social Sciences should establish a working group of experts in survey research, empirical social science, and military subject matter charged with development of a new longitudinal survey strategy to track both individuals and small units over time.

REFERENCE

U.S. Office of Management and Budget. (2013). Circular No. A-11 Preparation, Submission, and Execution of the Budget. Executive Office of the President, July 2013. Available: http://www.whitehouse.gov/sites/default/files/omb/assets/a11_current_year/a11_2013.pdf [January 2014].

Appendix

Biographical Sketches of Committee Members and Staff

Reid Hastie (*Chair*) is Ralph and Dorothy Keller Distinguished Service professor of behavioral science in the Graduate School of Business at the University of Chicago. Previously, he held positions at Harvard University, Northwestern University, and the University of Colorado. His primary research interests are in the areas of judgment and decision making. He is the author (with Robyn Dawes) of *Rational Choice in an Uncertain World*, an overview of the field of judgment and decision making. Currently, he is studying the role of causal reasoning in judgments of many kinds: civil jury decision making (punitive damages, securities fraud); decision-making competencies across the adult life span; and writing a book (with Cass Sunstein) on how to amplify the "collective intelligence" of teams and other groups. He has a Ph.D. in psychology from Yale University.

Catherine H. Tinsley (*Vice Chair*) is professor of management at the McDonough School of Business at Georgetown University and executive director of the Georgetown University Women's Leadership Initiative. She studies how culture, reputations, gender, and other factors influence negotiation and conflict resolution. She also studies how people make decisions under risk, applying decision analytic frameworks to understand organizational disasters and individual and expert responses to natural disasters (such as hurricanes) and man-made disasters (terrorist attacks). She has received grants from NASA, the National Science Foundation, and the Department of Homeland Security for work on decision making and risk and grants from the Department of Defense and Army Research Office for modeling culture's influence on negotiation and collaboration. She has won various academic awards for her research, which has appeared in numerous peer-reviewed journals. She is on the editorial board of *Organizational Behavior and Human Decision Processes, Negotiation and Conflict Management Research*, and the *International Journal of Conflict Management* and a former editorial board member of the *Academy of Management Journal*. She has a B.A. in anthropology from Bryn Mawr College and an M.A. and Ph.D. in organizational behavior from J.L. Kellogg Graduate School of Management at Northwestern University.

Burt S. Barnow is the Amsterdam professor of public service and economics in the Trachtenberg School of Public Policy and Public Administration at George Washington University. He has over 30 years of experience as an economist and manager of research projects in the fields of workforce development, program evaluation, performance analysis, labor economics, welfare, poverty, child support, and fatherhood initiatives. He has extensive experience conducting research on implementation and effectiveness of large government programs. Current and recent research projects include developing and evaluating demonstrations that test innovative strategies to promote self-sufficiency for low-income families for the U.S. Department of Health and Human Services and an evaluation of the Accelerating Opportunity demonstration, which is testing new strategies for linking adult education and vocational training. Formerly, he was associate director for research at Johns Hopkins University's Institute for Policy Studies, where he worked for 18 years. He has also worked for the Lewin Group, U.S. Department of Labor (including 4 years as Director of the Office of Research and Evaluation in the Employment and Training Administration), and the University of Pittsburgh. He is an elected member of the National Academy of Social Insurance and elected fellow of the National Academy of Public Administration. He has a B.S. in economics from the Massachusetts Institute of Technology and an M.S. and a Ph.D. in economics from the University of Wisconsin–Madison.

Corinne Bendersky is associate professor of management and organizations at the University of California, Los Angeles, Anderson School of Management. She studies the effects of workplace conflict, status, and justice on group and organizational performance. Her research aims to understand how phenomena that are generally studied in isolation and/or as static constructs function differently when they are examined in group and organizational contexts and as dynamically evolving processes. Her contextualized and dynamic perspectives surface overlooked and sometimes counterintuitive findings about these fundamental aspects of organizations. Her research has appeared in many journals and edited books. She is on the editorial review boards of the *Academy of Management Journal* and *Small*

Group Research. Dr. Bendersky is an experienced mediator, facilitator of group decisions, and developer of interpersonal leadership skills. She has also helped organizations evaluate and develop effective dispute resolution systems. She received her B.A. from Oberlin College and her Ph.D. from the Massachusetts Institute of Technology Sloan School of Management.

Cherie Chauvin (*Study Director*) is a senior program officer at the National Research Council, working on numerous studies relevant to defense, national security, and intelligence issues. She has served as the Study Director for projects answering the needs of the Office of the Director of National Intelligence, U.S. Department of Homeland Security, Office of Naval Research, and U.S Army Research Institute for the Behavioral and Social Sciences, and she has contributed to studies for the U.S Army's National Ground Intelligence Center, National Institute for Occupational Safety and Health, and the Federal Aviation Administration. Previously, she was an intelligence officer with the U.S. Department of Defense's Defense Intelligence Agency (DIA), where her work included support for military operations and liaison relationships across Sub-Saharan Africa and in Japan, South Korea, and Mongolia, as well as conducting worldwide intelligence collection operations (including during deployment to Afghanistan) to answer strategic and tactical military intelligence requirements. In recognition of her service, she was awarded the DIA Civilian Expeditionary Medal, the Department of the Army Commander's Award for Civilian Service, and the Office of the Director of National Intelligence National Meritorious Unit Citation. She holds a B.S. in cognitive science from the University of California at San Diego, an M.A. in international relations from The Maxwell School at Syracuse University, and an M.S. in strategic intelligence from the National Defense Intelligence College.

Edward J. Coss is associate professor of military history at the U.S. Army Command and General Staff College (Ft. Belvoir branch). He has written and presented papers dealing with soldier motivation and behavior at dozens of worldwide conferences. His work, *All for the King's Shilling: The British Soldier under Wellington, 1808-1814*, deals with the internal and external forces that affected the behavior of the British regulars. The work won the Literary Prize (1st place) from the International Napoleonic Society in 2010 and was runner-up for the Templer Award from the Society of Army Historical Research (London). He was nominated and selected as a Fellow of the Royal Historical Society in 2011. He is also a member of both the United States Commission on Military History and the British Commission for Military History. In 2010 he was named the Army's Civilian Educator of the Year. He received a Ph.D in history from The Ohio State University.

Leslie DeChurch is associate professor of organizational psychology at the Georgia Institute of Technology. Her research interests include leadership and teamwork in organizations. She leads the Georgia Tech Developing Effective Leaders, Teams, and Alliances research group, which conducts high-impact scientific projects that yield novel insights into effective organization with real-world impact. Some current questions include: What makes effective team leaders? How do teams successfully collaborate across boundaries? How are leadership and team dynamics sustained in virtual organizations? Her research has appeared in leading peer-reviewed journals, and she serves on the editorial boards of the *Journal of Applied Psychology, Small Group Research, Journal of Occupational and Organizational Psychology,* and the *Journal of Business and Psychology*. In 2011 she received a National Science Foundation (NSF) CAREER award to study leadership in virtual organizations; in 2012 she received an NSF Research Coordination Network project grant (with Noshir Contractor) to leverage big data for the advancement of computational social science. She currently studies leadership networks and multiteam systems and teaches social psychology, including social networks. She earned a B.S. in environmental science from the University of Miami, Coral Gables, and an M.S. and Ph.D. in industrial and organizational psychology from Florida International University in Miami.

Jonathan Gratch is research professor of computer science and psychology at the University of Southern California (USC), director for virtual human research at UCS's Institute for Creative Technologies, and co-director of USC's Computational Emotion Group. His research focuses on computational models of human cognitive and social processes, especially emotion, and explores these models' role in shaping human-computer interactions in virtual environments. He studies the relationship between cognition and emotion, the cognitive processes underlying emotional responses, and the influence of emotion on decision making and physical behavior. He is the founding and current editor-in-chief of the Institute of Electrical and Electronics Engineers' (IEEE) *Transactions on Affective Computing; associate editor of Emotion Review and the Journal of Autonomous Agents and Multiagent Systems*; former president of the Association for the Advancement of Affective Computing, and a fellow of the Association for the Advancement of Artificial Intelligence, a senior member of IEEE, and a member of the International Society for Research on Emotion. He is the author of over 250 technical articles. He earned a Ph.D. in computer science at the University of Illinois in Urbana-Champaign.

Douglas H. Harris is chairman and principal scientist at Anacapa Sciences, Inc., a research company he formed in 1969 to enhance human performance in complex systems and organizations. In addition to completing projects involving business, government, educational, and military entities and operations, he has conducted workshops and training courses in Canada, Mexico, Serbia, Singapore, Sweden, the United Kingdom, the United States, and Venezuela. He is a fellow and past president of the Human Factors and Ergonomics Society, fellow of the American Psychological Association, and charter fellow of the Association for Psychological Science. His formal training is in psychology, statistics, engineering, and military science. He served in the U.S. Navy as the operations officer of Underwater Demolition Team 11, planning and leading operations in Asia. He has contributed to many research and advisory activities, addressing issues involving human factors, organizational productivity, soldier systems, aviation security, airport passenger screening, and assessment of threat communications. He has a Ph.D. in industrial psychology from Purdue University.

Lee D. Hoffer is associate professor of anthropology at Case Western Reserve University. His research focuses on understanding the political, social, cultural, and clinical contexts related to illicit drug use, with emphasis on applying field-collected data to computational and agent-based models and complex-system behavioral models. His research synthesizes agent-based computational modeling techniques and ethnographic research to develop new tools for policy makers and researchers. Borrowing from theories of complexity systems, these projects seek to connect the rich descriptive detail offered by anthropology with the epidemiology of drug abuse. His research has application to HIV risk behaviors, diagnostic nosology for substance use disorders, understanding trends in drug use, and drug policy and intervention. Recent research examines how illicit drug markets and the acquisition of drugs influence behaviors and negative health outcomes. From 1997 to 1999 he was Colorado's representative to the National Institute on Drug Abuse (NIDA) Community Epidemiology Workgroup. He was also active in the Colorado Department of Public Health and Environment and the Centers for Disease Control and Prevention HIV community planning efforts. From 2002 to 2005 he trained as a (T32) NIDA postdoctoral fellow in psychiatric epidemiology at Washington University School of Medicine in St. Louis, Epidemiology and Prevention Research Group. He has an M.A. in anthropology and a Ph.D. in health and behavioral sciences from the University of Colorado in Denver and a master of psychiatric epidemiology from Washington University School of Medicine in St. Louis.

Alair MacLean is associate professor of sociology at Washington State University Vancouver. Her research focuses broadly on social inequality. She is currently exploring the question of how wars affect people's lives. In this research, she examines the life course trajectories of veterans who served in the U.S. armed forces, focusing on the effects of military service and combat exposure on work and health. She has published articles in peer-reviewed journals and is a member of the American Sociological Association, the Population Association of America, and the Inter-University Seminar on Armed Forces and Society. She received an M.S. and Ph.D. in sociology at the University of Wisconsin-Madison and completed a postdoctoral fellowship at the RAND Corporation.

Charles F. Manski has been Board of Trustees professor in economics at Northwestern University since 1997. He was previously a faculty member at the University of Wisconsin-Madison, the Hebrew University of Jerusalem, and Carnegie Mellon University. His research spans econometrics, judgment and decision, and the analysis of social policy. He has authored six monographs in these fields, and has co-authored or co-edited additional monographs. He was director of the Institute for Research on Poverty and chair of the Board of Overseers of the Panel Study of Income Dynamics, as well as editor of the *Journal of Human Resources*, co-editor of the *Econometric Society Monograph Series*, member of the editorial board of the *Annual Review of Economics*, and associate editor of the *Annals of Applied Statistics*, *Econometrica*, *Journal of Economic Perspectives*, *Journal of the American Statistical Association*, and *Transportation Science*. He is an elected member of the National Academy of Sciences and an elected fellow of the Econometric Society, the American Academy of Arts and Sciences, and the American Association for the Advancement of Science. He received a B.S. and a Ph.D. in economics from the Massachusetts Institute of Technology.

William D. Schulze is the Kenneth L. Robinson professor of agricultural economics and public policy at Cornell University. His areas of research include environmental, public, experimental, and behavioral economics. Recent and ongoing research includes studies funded by the U.S. Environmental Protection Agency on the benefits of air pollution control, including air toxics, and an analysis of the impact of the Superfund program. Current research also includes a National Science Foundation–sponsored study of the validity of survey methods for valuing the benefits of environmental programs. Much of his work explores environmental values and the development of demand-revealing mechanisms using both the experimental laboratory and survey research. Current experimental economics research includes efforts to develop private mechanisms for funding public goods and markets for electric power. He has a B.A. from San Diego State College and a Ph.D. in economics from the University of California, Riverside.

Tina Winters is an associate program officer at the National Research Council, where she has played an integral part in dozens of studies over a career spanning 20 years. She currently is a staff member for the Board on Behavioral, Cognitive, and Sensory Sciences and previously worked on consensus studies and other activities related to K-12 science and mathematics education, testing and assessment, education research, and social science research for public policy use. She was a co-editor of *Advancing Scientific Research in Education.*